Ma¹¹ι

FRANCE

ITALY

SPAIN

CORSICA

MALLORCA

SARDINIA

Mediterranean Sea

ALGERIA

TUNISIA

HarperCollins*Publishers*

YOUR COLLINS TRAVELLER

Your Collins Traveller Guide will help you find your way around your chosen destination quickly and easily. It is colour-coded for easy reference:

The blue section answers the question 'I would like to see or do something; where do I go and what do I see when I get there?' This section is arranged as an alphabetical list of topics and it is recommended that an up-to-date atlas or street plan is used in conjunction with their location maps. Within each topic you will find:
- A selection of the best examples on offer.
- How to get there, costs and opening hours for each entry.
- The outstanding features of each entry.
- A simplified map, with each entry plotted and the nearest landmark or transport access.

The red section is a lively and informative gazetteer. It offers:
- Essential facts about the main places and cultural items.
  What is La Bastille? Who was Michelangelo? Where is Delphi?

The gold section is full of practical and invaluable travel information. It offers:
- Everything you need to know to help you enjoy yourself and get the most out of your time away, from Accommodation through Baby-sitters, Car Hire, Food, Health, Money, Newspapers, Taxis, Telephones to Youth Hostels.

PRICES	Inexpensive	Moderate	Expensive
Attractions Museums, etc.	under 300 ptas	300-700 ptas	over 700 ptas
Restaurants Main courses	under 2000 ptas	2000-4000 ptas	over 4000 ptas
Nightlife Dinner & show	under 2000 ptas	2000-5000 ptas	over 5000 ptas

Cross-references:

Type in small capitals – CHURCHES – tells you that more information on an item is available within the topic on churches.

A-Z after an item tells you that more information is available within the gazetteer. Simply look under the appropriate name.

A name in bold – **Holy Cathedral** – also tells you that more information on an item is available in the gazetteer – again simply look up the name.

CONTENTS

CONTENTS

▨ PRACTICAL INFORMATION GAZETTEER

INTRODUCTION

Mallorca, or Majorca, is the largest of Spain's Balearic Islands (its name comes from the Latin *major*). Since earliest times its position on Mediterranean trade routes between Spain and the East made it an important centre visited by Phoenicians, Greeks and Carthaginians. Roman attempts at invasion eventually succeeded in 123 BC. Later it became part of the Byzantine Empire in the 6thC and, in AD 902, was invaded by the Moors who already dominated most of mainland Spain. In 1229 Mallorca was again conquered, this time by Jaume I, King of Aragon, who repopulated it with Christians mainly from Catalunya, thus introducing Catalan, which remains the first language of the islanders.

Today, Mallorca is the most popular holiday destination, in terms of numbers, in the European package holiday industry. Every year about five million tourists, mainly British and German, arrive at Palma airport, one of Europe's busiest, while another half a million step off ferries from Spain and elsewhere. What's the attraction? Undeniably the assurance of fine summer weather and good beaches, plus the fact that a wide variety of accommodation, food, entertainment and leisure facilities is available at hard-to-beat prices.

Despite the numbers, it is a fallacy that mass tourism has scarred Mallorca with a concrete jungle of huge hotels and brash resorts. In fact, large-scale developments have mainly been confined to the bay of Palma. These resorts, like Magaluf and Arenal, remain unbeatable in terms of price. Elsewhere on the island, however, most resorts are smaller and quieter.

Long before the tourist boom started in the 1950s, Mallorca had its ardent aficionados. From the end of the last century artists and writers began to settle on the island, among them the Austrian Archduke Ludwig Salvator, who wrote a nine-volume study of the Balearics, and the English poet and novelist Robert Graves. Much of what charmed them still remains. Pockets of rural life and inland villages are undisturbed; fishing communities, though depleted, continue to land their catches, and the beautiful scenery and stunning seascapes remain unspoilt.

By the 1920s an up-market tourist industry was emerging with the opening of the luxurious Hotel Formentor. Since then, a number of

Poble Espanyol, Palma

beautiful old country houses have been converted into high-class hotels, and the wealthy yachting fraternity continues to moor at expensive marinas. The strongest evidence that Mallorca's up-market holiday element is still flourishing is the presence each summer of Spain's royal family at their holiday home on the island.

Tourism is now the island's lifeblood and Mallorca continues to keep up with new trends in the industry. Time-share and self-catering villas and apartments are increasingly available and are now usually built in a style in keeping with traditional buildings. Evidence that care and thought goes into catering for tourists ranges from good facilities for families with children and people with disabilities at many newer developments to safe cycle lanes in a number of resorts.

The island offers plenty of opportunities for activities other than sunbathing. Water sports and boat trips are family favourites, while sailing and tennis facilities are also widely available. Other healthy pursuits could range from a gentle walk or horse ride through the picturesque countryside to strenuous hiking and mountain climbing. Experienced cyclists enjoy testing themselves on the steep mountain roads of the

Formentor

northwest, while less experienced ones wobble in family groups along flat areas like the bay of Alcúdia. Bird-watchers and botanists will not be disappointed, particularly if they visit S'Albufera in the north or the salt flats in the southeast. Golfers are increasingly attracted by good all-year-round weather and courses with high-quality facilities in beautiful settings. Throughout the year Mallorca has much to offer. In spring the countryside is at its prettiest, while autumn is like a good North European summer. Winters are mild and many older people go for long-stay breaks.

Sightseeing highlights are numerous in the island's capital, Palma de Mallorca, which was voted the best place to live in the whole of Spain in a survey by the Spanish newspaper *El País* in 1991. It is a sophisticated city of narrow, evocative streets and elegant buildings, dominated by the imposing Gothic cathedral. Sights around the island include spectacular limestone caves, isolated monasteries, medieval fortifications, and *talaiots*, stone structures built by Mallorca's Bronze-Age inhabitants. Most of all, however, it's the attractive scenery, especially in the mountainous northwest, which makes the island a sightseeing delight.

Palma has a good choice of shops, from up-market designer clothes shops and craft workshops to bustling traditional markets. Many resorts

also have a good range of shops and arts and crafts galleries, and every village has its weekday market. Craftsmen can be seen making items for sale. Blown glass, artificial pearls and leather goods can be good buys. Cultural life is inevitably centred on Palma's museums, art centres and theatres but throughout the island there are a number of important summer festivals of music. The innumerable traditional local festivals provide a fascinating opportunity to discover authentic island culture and customs.

Big tourist hotels and many restaurants play safe with bland international menus but traditional island cooking, such as tasty dishes of fresh local fish, or *tumbet*, a delicious vegetable dish, is also widely available at good prices. Increasingly, restaurants are offering imaginative versions of the new, lighter style of Mediterranean cooking, often adapting from old Mallorcan recipes. Nightlife in the resorts centres on late-night bars and discotheques. In Magaluf there's the extraordinary BCM, as well as the casino with its own nightclub. Palma's Es Terreno district has the best variety. Barbecues, with shows of Spanish dancing or medieval tournaments, are other options. But on Mallorca's balmy nights there's a strong temptation to do no more than sit on a terrace or by the beach, sipping the local wine.

Catedral, Palma

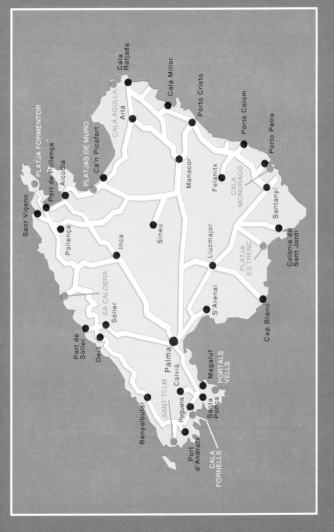

PORTALS VELLS Boat excursion from Palma (Passeig Maritim-Auditòrium), Magaluf (Hotel Trinidad) and Cala d'Or.
Easy access from Magaluf. To the south, and less developed, is Cala Figuera (see A-Z). Go through pine woods to tiny Platja Mago, the island's official nudist beach.

CALA FORNELLS
Peaceful beach near resorts of Santa Ponça, Peguera and Camp de Mar.

SANT TELM Boat excursions from Palma, Peguera (Hotel Mar i Pins), Port d'Andratx and Port de Sóller.
Facing Dragonera island, a pretty cove with a fine sand beach and rocks.

SA CALOBRA Boat excursions from Port de Sóller (see **EXCURSION 4**). Access via a switchback road which is not for the faint-hearted.
You can swim either in the sea or the Torrent de Pareis's fresh water.

PLATJA ES TRENC
Between Colònia de Sant Jordi and Sa Ràpita.
A stretch of fine sand with pines, dunes and good amenities. Some unofficial nudism.

PLATJA FORMENTOR
Boat excursions from Port de Pollença and Port d'Alcúdia.
A pine-backed beach of silken sand. See **EXCURSION 2**.

PLATJAS DE MURO
A thin ribbon of gently sloping fine sand backed by shady pines.

CALA AGULLA
Good amenities, some sand dunes and a protected stretch of beach. The more isolated Cala Mesquida is a short hike to the north.

CALA MONDRAGÓ
Convenient for Cala d'Or (see A-Z) and Porto Petro, this relatively undeveloped cove has beach amenities and two good bars.

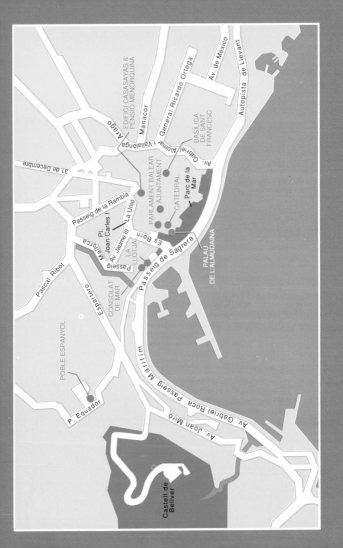

CATEDRAL c/ Palau Reial 29.
■ 1000-1630 Mon.-Fri., 1000-1330 Sat. Closed hols. ● Inexpensive.
Gothic cathedral (also called La Seo) of impressive dimensions, begun just after the island's conquest by Jaume I in 1229. See **WALK 1**, **A-Z**.

PALAU DE L'ALMUDAINA c/ Palau Reial s/n. ■ 1000-1900
Mon.-Fri., 1000-1330 Sat. & hols (summer). Guided tours. ● Moderate.
Free to EC members Wed. *The royal palace, originally built by the Moors (see* **A-Z**) *but altered by Philip II in the 16thC. See* **WALKS 1 & 2**.

BASÍLICA DE SANT FRANCESC Plaça Sant Francesc 7.
■ 0930-1300, 1530-1845 Mon.-Sat., 0930-1300 Sun. & hols.
● Inexpensive. *Gothic church with Baroque façade, tomb of Ramon Llull (see* **A-Z**) *and attractive cloister. See* **WALK 1**.

LA LLOTJA Passeig de Sagrera s/n. ■ 1100-1400, 1700-2100 Tue.-
Sat., 1100-1400 Sun. & hols. ● Inexpensive. *The 15thC merchants' exchange, designed by Guillem Sagrera. Excellent example of Spanish Gothic civic architecture. Used for modern art exhibitions. See* **WALK 2**.

CONSOLAT DE MAR Passeig de Sagrera s/n. ■ Exterior only.
17thC shipping exchange; now houses island's autonomous government.

POBLE ESPANYOL c/ Poble Espanyol 39. ■ Craft workshops 1000-
1800 Mon.-Sat. *Replicas of famous Spanish buildings. See* **SHOPPING 3**.

AJUNTAMENT Plaça Cort. ■ Exterior only.
The town hall has an attractive 17thC Baroque façade. See **WALK 1**.

PARLAMENT BALEAR Costa del Conquistador II. ■ 0900-1300
Mon.-Fri. ● Free. *19thC building of Círculo Mallorquín with Modernista (see* **A-Z**) *façade. Now houses parliament of autonomous government.*

EDIFICI CASASAYAS & PENSIÓ MENORQUINA

Plaça del Mercat 13-14. ■ Shops on ground floor; refurbished interior.
Palma's best example of Modernista (see **A-Z**) *architecture.*

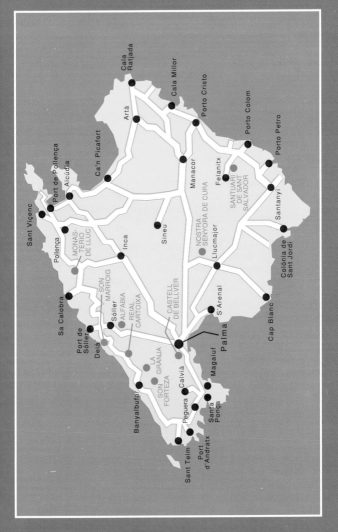

MONASTERIO DE LLUC Escorça. ▥ 1000-1900. Museum 1000-1830. ● Museum; Inexpensive. Monastery; Free.
*The island's principal monastery in a barren mountain setting. Pilgrims venerate the statue of the Virgin of Lluc, patroness of the island. The boys' choir, Els Blavets (see **A-Z**), sings at 1115.*

NOSTRA SENYORA DE CURA Ctra Algaida-Llucmajor. ● Free.
*Small monastery where Ramon Llull (see **A-Z**) began the ascetic life. There are good views of Mount Randa.*

SANTUARI DE SANT SALVADOR Ctra Felinitx-Porto Colom. ● Free. *Picture-book monastery from the 14thC. Panoramic views.*

SON MARROIG Deià. ▥ 0930-1400, 1630-2000 Mon.-Sat. (summer). ● Moderate. *The mansion of Archduke Ludwig Salvator (see **A-Z**), housing his art collections, library and memorabilia. Beautiful views from the mirador. See* **MUSIC**.

REIAL CARTOIXA (REAL CARTUJA) Valldemossa. ▥ 0930-1330, 1500-1900 Mon.-Sat. ● Expensive. *Includes the Carthusian monastery where Chopin (see **A-Z**) and George Sand stayed, and 14thC Palau del Rei Sanxo. See* **MUSEUMS 2, MUSIC, Valldemossa**.

LA GRANJA Esporles. ▥ 1000-1900 summer. ● Expensive.
*Country house of Fortuny family and Mallorcan heritage centre. See **A-Z**.*

ALFABIA Ctra Bunyola-Sóller. ▥ 0930-1900 May-Oct., 0930-1730 Nov.-April. ● Inexpensive. *Visit here principally for the gardens laid out in Moorish style. See* **EXCURSION 1, Jardins de Alfabia**.

SON FORTEZA Puigpunyent. ▥ Exterior only. ● Free.
A fine example of the many country houses of important island families.

CASTELL DE BELLVER Above Es Terreno.
▥ 0800-2000 summer. Closed hols. ● Inexpensive.
14thC castle with circular courtyard. Views of Palma bay. See **MUSIC**.

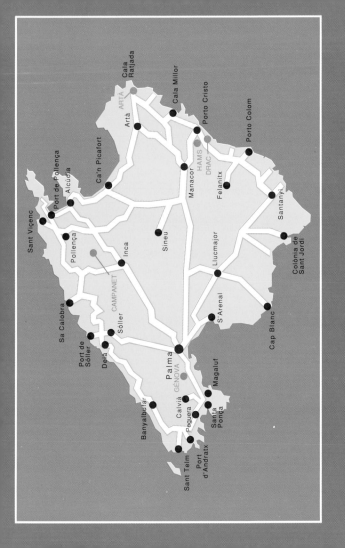

DRAC Porto Cristo, tel: 820753.

▨ Guided tour with concert. 1000-1200, 1400-1700 (on the hour) summer; 1045, 1200, 1400, 1530 (and without concert 1630) winter. ● Expensive.

Drac means 'dragon' in Mallorquin. Crowds flock to join the guided tours of Mallorca's best-known caves. Stalagmites and stalactites with imaginative names are beautifully lit. A sound-and-light concert across the long and deep Lago Martell provides a memorable finale. No photographs permitted. If you're not going with a coach tour, telephone ahead to check availability of places.

HAMS Porto Cristo, tel: 820988.

▨ Guided tours with concert every 15 min. 1030-1315, 1415-1615 summer; 1030-1315, 1415-1515 winter. ● Expensive.

Named after the fish-hook formations in the Angel's Dream cavern. Smaller than the nearby Coves del Drac but no less fascinating in the variety of formations, caverns and illuminations. A brief lake-side concert is included. A socavón show with flamenco, regional and classical dancing is held at 2130 Sun. (June-Sep.).

ARTÀ Platja de Canyamel, 9 km southeast of Artà. Tel: 563293.

▨ 0930-1900 summer, 0930-1700 winter. ● Moderate.

Said to have inspired Jules Verne's Journey to the Centre of the Earth. *A limestone headland eroded by water with caverns 300 m deep and 45 m high. Enter through a huge slit in the cliff. Steep walking inside. See* EXCURSION 3.

CAMPANET Near Campanet, off Ctra Palma-Alcúdia. Tel: 516130.

▨ 1000-1900 summer, 1000-1800 winter. ● Expensive.

Fewer tourists visit these small inland caves, although they have well-illuminated rock formations.

GÉNOVA Génova, tel: 402387.

▨ 1000-1300, 1600-1900. ● Moderate.

Tiny by comparison with the others but very conveniently located near Palma and the Palma bay resorts.

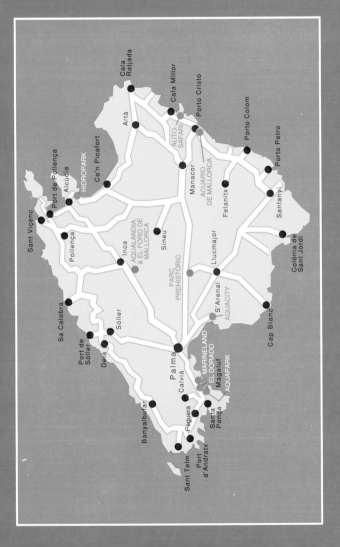

AQUACITY S'Arenal. At end of motorway. ■ 1000-1730 May-Oct.
Bus 23 every 20 min from Plaça Espanya, Palma. ● Moderate.
One of the largest water funfairs in the world.

AQUAPARK Ctra Cala Figuera-Magaluf.
■ 1000-1700 May, June & Oct., 1000-1800 July-Sep. ● Expensive.
Long-established and well maintained. Water slides and lots of thrills.

AQUALANDIA & EL FORO DE MALLORCA Ctra Palma-Inca.
North of Binissalem. ■ 1000-1730. ● Inexpensive.
Water slide, swimming pool, mini-golf, waxworks, crafts and souvenirs.

HIDROPARK Avinguda Inglaterra, Port d'Alcúdia, tel: 547072.
■ 1000-1900. ● Expensive.
Good water funfair, including facilities for the very young.

MARINELAND Costa d'en Blanes. ■ 1030-1845. ● Expensive.
*Popular shows with performing dolphins, sea lions and parrots, though
some visitors may find the displays distasteful.*

ACUARIO DE MALLORCA Next to Coves del Drac, Porto Cristo.
■ 0900-1900. ● Moderate.
Small aquarium with exotic fish from around the world.

AUTO-SAFARI Ctra Porto Cristo-Son Servera.
■ 0900-1900 summer, 0900-1700 winter. ● Moderate.
*A 4 km drive by car or mini-train through meadowland where elephants,
rhinos, giraffes, zebras, antelopes, deer and monkeys roam.*

EL DORADO Ctra Cala Figuera-Magaluf. ■ Show 1200 daily.
Visits 1300-1900 Mon.-Sat., 1300-1500 Sun. ● Expensive.
Wild West attraction, including restaurants, shops and show.

PARC PREHISTÒRIC Ctra Palma-Manacor, near Algaida.
■ 1000-2000. ● Inexpensive.
30 life-size models in a pine-wood park with lake and waterfalls.

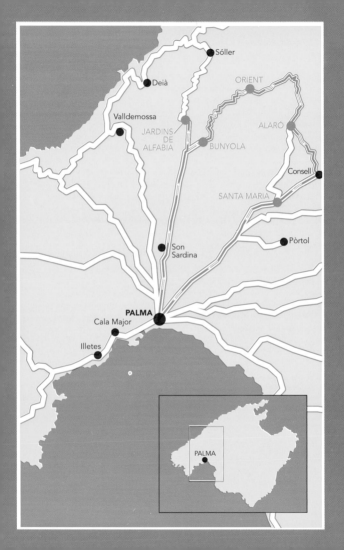

A half-day excursion from Palma to the nearby mountains and villages.

Take the C 711 out of Palma, signposted Sóller. Pass the turn-off for Bunyola after 14 km. Turn right 4 km further on to the Jardins de Alfabia.

18 km – Jardins de Alfabia (see BUILDINGS 2, **A-Z**). At the foot of the mountainous Serra de Alfabia and irrigated by water from the mountain streams, these delightful gardens are laid out in Moorish style.

24 km – Bunyola. Take care at the level crossing over the Palma–Sóller railway line (no gates). As the road climbs up into the village, there are good views across the wooded valley to the mountains. On the left is one of the distilleries of the liqueur *palo*, for which Bunyola is famous (see **Drinks**). The main square is dominated by the parish church and library, and around it are several cafés. The route continues uphill opposite the main square (signposted Orient/Alaró), veering left at the little square at the top. This is the PM 210 which has splendid mountain views but also some sharp bends on the steep ascent.

35 km – Orient. Situated high in the mountains, 400 m above sea level, this village is one of the most picturesque spots on the island. Steps lead up to the parish church, from which is a magnificent panorama of the village and mountains. Continuing on the PM 210 past, on the left, The Hermitage country house hotel and restaurant, the road begins to descend through olive groves. High above on the right perch the ruins of Castell d'Alaró, a stronghold of the Moors (see **A-Z**) until 1231, two years after the conquest of the island by Jaume I (see **A-Z**). A road on the right, 8 km after Orient, leads up to the castle and tiny chapel but it is not recommended for cars.

45 km – Alaró. A market village near the foot of the *serra* with some narrow streets of attractive stone houses and views over the rolling agricultural countryside. Continue on the PM 210 and at Consell turn right onto the C 713, signposted Santa Maria/Palma.

50 km – Santa Maria. In the centre of the village are the 16thC Convent dels Minimos, with a costume collection in its cloisters (tel: 620174 to arrange a visit), and the Baroque parish church. Leave Santa Maria on the C 713 and after 5 km join the motorway (PM 7), signposted Autovia/Palma, for the last 10 km.

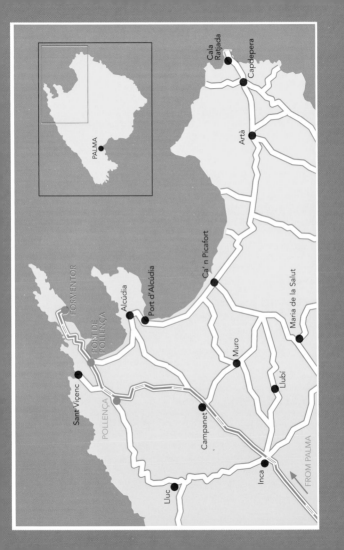

A one-day excursion to Pollença and Formentor.

Take the PM 7 motorway (which becomes the C 713), signposted Autovia/Inca. Continue on the C 713 12 km past Inca and turn left at the roundabout onto the PM 220, signposted Pollença. Approaching Pollença, turn left at one of the signs marked Centre.

54 km – Pollença (see A-Z). Just below the main square, on c/ Santo Domingo, is the Claustre de Santo Domingo (see MUSEUMS 2), originally a Dominican monastery which now houses the municipal museum and is the venue for a summer music festival (see MUSIC). Following c/ Antoni Maura up into Plaça Major, ahead is the elegant building of the Club Pollença which serves refreshments. Around the square are other cafés and eating places, and the principal parish church. Uphill behind the church is the Calvari, a climb of 365 steps to a 19thC chapel with an image of the Virgin possibly dating from the 13thC (the ascent can also be made by road). On the higher hill of Puig de Maria is the Santuari, a small hermitage and 14thC chapel accessible by car or foot up a twisting road off the main PM 220 Palma–Pollença road. To the north, just off the C 710 to Lluc/Sóller, is the Pont Roma (Roman Bridge), though it was probably built by the Vandals in the 5thC AD. Continue on the PM 220, signposted Port de Pollença at the roundabout.

60 km – Port de Pollença (see RESORTS 2, A-Z). Turn left onto the PM 221, signposted Formentor, where the beach and cafés with terraces may prove tempting. The road begins to climb and twist steeply above the bay of Pollença through rugged and rocky landscapes. After 6 km there is parking at the Mirador d'es Colomer, a lookout point with splendid views along Cape Formentor. From here, the road winds down to the bay of Formentor. The main road turns sharp left and continues for another 11 km to Formentor point and lighthouse. On the way are two smaller miradors with parking space, a short tunnel through the limestone rock and several hairpin bends. Returning to Formentor bay, turn left at the signpost for Hotel Formentor and visit the famous luxurious hotel to take refreshments on its terrace, wander through its exotic gardens or down to Platja Formentor (see BEACHES). Return to Palma via the route as before.

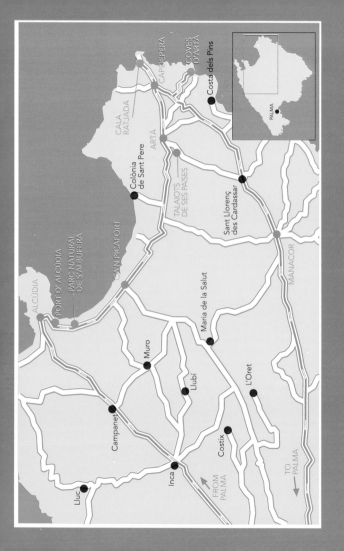

A two-day excursion from Palma (with an overnight stop at Port d'Alcúdia) round the bay of Alcúdia.

Follow the same route as for **EXCURSION 2** as far as the roundabout 12 km past Inca, and from there continue on the C 713 to Alcúdia.
53 km – Alcúdia (see **A-Z**). With several of its gates and stretches of its medieval walls still standing, Alcúdia presents an imposing sight. At the first gate (Port de Mallorca) turn right and park to visit the town on foot. Ahead is the massive, late-Gothic parish church of Sant Jaume (1000-1300, 1700-2000 Tue.-Fri., 1000-1300 Sat. & Sun.; Free) with a large Renaissance side chapel and cupola. A huge Baroque altarpiece frames the simple 15thC figure of Christ on the Cross. Behind the church is the Museu Monogràfic de Pollentia (see **MUSEUMS 2**), a small but fascinating museum devoted to the history of Urbs Pollentia (the Roman name for Alcúdia) and containing finds from local excavations. c/ Sant Jaume leads into the town's narrow streets, where there are a number of *casa senyorales* (noblemen's houses). At No. 7 in c/ Albellons (left off c/ Sant Jaume) is the Bryant Foundation which funds excavations. Turn right past the town hall with its Baroque clock tower to reach the main square, Plaça de la Constitució, with small shops and a café crowded during the Thu. and Sun. markets. Turn right down c/ d'en Serra to emerge onto the main ring road at a section of the city walls just below the church of Sant Jaume. Continuing by car, turn left at the traffic lights by the church. Immediately on the left are parking spaces for visiting the Roman site (open access; Free), excavated in 1961, of two houses dating from the 1stC AD. At the first and larger house, the layout of rooms round the atrium or courtyard with pool and columns can be distinguished. Continue on to Port d'Alcúdia (68 km) (see **RESORTS 2**) and turn right onto the C 712 to follow the wide, sweeping bay of Alcúdia. From the harbour stretches the long beach of Platja d'Alcúdia, lined with hotels and cafés. On the right is the artificial lake Estany Esperança. Half a kilometre past the turn-off for Sa Pobla turn right, signposted S'Albufera, to visit the nature reserve.
73 km – Parc Natural de S'Albufera (see **A-Z**). 0900-1900 summer, 0900-1700 winter; Free. A haven of tranquillity to be explored at a leisurely pace on foot, the wetlands reserve offers a stark contrast to the

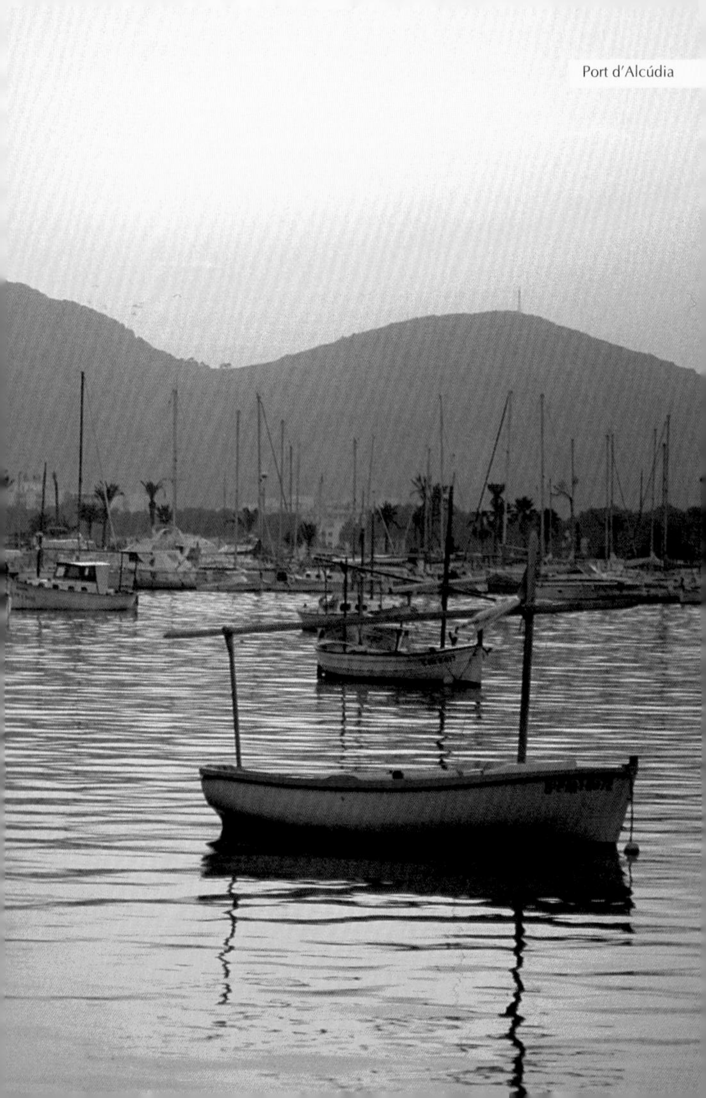

Port d'Alcúdia

resort development literally on its doorstep. The landscape of reeds, rushes, streams and sand dunes provides a habitat for over 200 species of native and migratory birds. Among the pine woods several species of orchid grow. Continue along the C 712, passing on the right the camp site Camping Platja Blava (see **Camping**) before Ca'n Picafort (see RESORTS 2, **A-Z**). From here, the road veers inland and the landscape again becomes mountainous on the approach to Artà.

101 km – Artà (see **A-Z**). An attractive hill town dominated by the church of Sant Salvador on the site of the Moorish fortress. On entering Artà, turn left uphill to visit the church and ramparts, with wide views over the town and countryside. Inside the church (1000-1300, 1600-1900 Mon.-Fri., 1000-1300 Sat. & Sun.; Free) are early-20thC paintings of the conquest of Mallorca by Jaume I (see **A-Z**) and the martyrdom of Ramon Llull (see **A-Z**), a huge altarpiece framing an early image of the Virgin and Child, and a 15thC image of Christ on the Cross. Just below the fortress is the huge church of the Franciscan monastery, Convent d'Artà, with massive and unusual exterior arcades (open for Mass 0930 & 1800). Halfway down the hill on the left, in c/ Estrella, is the elegant Ajuntament (Town Hall) with a little interior courtyard and modern stained glass. To the right of it is the Museu Regional d'Artà (see MUSEUMS 2), containing important archaeological finds. Returning to the C 712, take the narrow road which runs south from it (signposted Ses Païsses) to visit the Bronze-Age site.

102 km – Talaiots (or **Talayots**) **de Ses Païsses.** Open access; Free. One of the most important of the many Bronze-Age *talaiots* (see **A-Z**) sites on the island, these huge stone monuments provide fascinating evidence of a settlement here between the 12th and 2ndC BC. This excursion could be extended with a visit to the hill town of Capdepera (see **A-Z**), the caves of Artà (see CAVES) and an overnight stop at the attractive resort of Cala Ratjada (see RESORTS 2, **A-Z**). Return to Palma via the C 715, passing through Manacor, famous for its pearls (see SHOPPING 3), and containing a small archaeological museum (see MUSEUMS 2).

EXCURSION 4

A one-day excursion by train, tram and boat to Sóller, Port de Sóller and Sa Colobra.

Train: From Palma to Sóller. Estació Sóller, c/ Eusebi Estada (off Plaça Espanya), Palma, tel: 752051. Timetables from station or tourist offices. Journey takes 1 hr. The special mid-morning train includes a photo-stop.

Opened in 1905 and electrified in 1929, the Palma–Sóller railway line is one of the most enjoyable train journeys anywhere. The old-style wooden carriages are hardly luxurious but are very quaint. When the train is ready to leave, the old-fashioned station bell is rung, the train whistles and then sets off creaking and rattling down the middle of the streets of Palma! Once out of the city, the train crosses the wide plain and begins the climb into the mountains, stopping at Bunyola (see **EXCURSION 1**) after 30 min. After a further climb, Sóller comes into view way below in the valley (photo-stop) and the train begins its descent among the delightful wooded and terraced slopes.
Sóller (see **A-Z**). Downhill from the station is the main square, Plaça Constitució, in which are the Ajuntament (Town Hall) with a tourist office, and a number of cafés. The parish church, Esglesia de Sant Bartomeu (1000-1230, 1430-1700 Mon.-Fri., 1000-1200 Sat.), original-ly dating from 1248, now has a mainly Baroque interior with interesting side chapels and a Modernista (see **A-Z**) façade by Joan Rubió i Bellver. Next door is the Banco Sóller by the same architect, with curious cob-web-like grilles on the windows. The pleasant, narrow streets off the square also repay a wander.

Tram: From Sóller railway station to Port de Sóller seafront. Half-hourly or hourly depending on the season and time of day. Timetables at tram stops and from tourist offices. Journey takes 20 min.

Just as much fun as the railway journey to Sóller is the 5 km by open San Francisco-style tram through agricultural countryside to palm-fringed Port de Sóller (see **RESORTS 2**, **A-Z**). The last stop is just by the pier, from where boats leave for Sa Calobra.

Boat: From Port de Sóller to Sa Calobra. Boat company: Barcos Azules. Timetables on the pier and from tourist offices, or tel: 630170/632061. Journey takes 50 min.

The exhilarating boat journey, with good views of the rugged coastline and mountains beyond, is the easiest way of reaching Sa Calobra, otherwise only accessible by the island's most tortuous (though spectacular) road. At Sa Calobra are restaurants, a small beach and the Torrent de Pareis, a gorge with 200 m sides worn by the rushing stream, undoubtedly one of the most stunning sights on the island. Exploration of the gorge itself is not recommended except with an experienced local guide. Tunnels lead to its little shingle beach. Return to Palma by boat, tram and train.

Port de Sóller

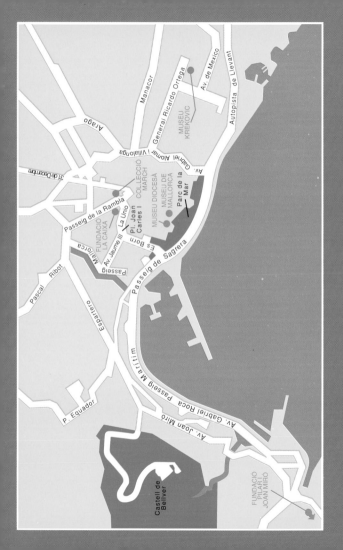

MUSEU DE MALLORCA c/ Portella 5.
■ 1000-1400, 1600-1900 Tue.-Fri., 1000-1400 Sat. & Sun.
● Inexpensive.
Archaeological items, medieval paintings, altarpieces and ceramics housed in the attractive late-Gothic Palau Ayamans. See **WALK 1**.

MUSEU DIOCESÀ c/ Mirador 7.
■ 1000-1330, 1500-2000 Mon.-Fri. (summer), 1000-1300, 1500-1800 Mon.-Fri. (winter); 1000-1330 Sat., Sun. & hols all year. ● Inexpensive.
Housed in the episcopal palace, an interesting collection of archaeology, Hispano-Moresque ceramics and glass, medieval paintings and sculpture, and fragments of architecture and decoration.

COL.LECCIÓ MARCH c/ Sant Miquel 11.
■ 1000-1330, 1430-1930 Mon.-Fri., 1000-1330 Sat. ● Inexpensive.
Important collection of 20thC Spanish art, including works by Picasso, Miró (see **A-Z**), *Dalí, Tàpies and Miquel Barceló. Housed in the first bank opened by the financier and important art patron Joan March.*

FUNDACIÓ PILAR I JOAN MIRÓ c/ Joan de Saridakis 29, Cala Major.
■ Open 1992. Contact tourist office for opening times and prices.
The studios of the important 20thC artist Joan Miró (see **A-Z**) *who settled here in 1940. Permanent collection and changing exhibitions.*

FUNDACIÓ LA CAIXA Gran Hotel, Plaça Weyler.
■ Open 1993. Contact tourist office for opening times and prices.
A centre of Modernista (see **A-Z**) *art, including a collection of paintings by Anglada i Camarasa (see* **A-Z**) *who settled in Port de Pollença.*

MUSEU KREKOVIC c/ Ciutat de Querétaro 3, Poligon de Llevant.
■ 1030-1300, 1500-1800 Mon.-Fri., 1000-1300 Sat. ● Inexpensive.
Vivid paintings by Croatian painter (1901-85) depicting themes of the Incas, Peru and Hispano-America.

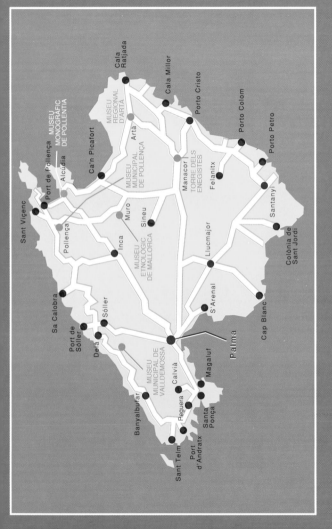

MUSEU MUNICIPAL DE VALLDEMOSSA

Reial Cartoixa (Real Cartuja), Valldemossa.
▓ 0930-1330, 1500-1900 Mon.-Sat. (summer). ● Expensive.
*Exhibits relating to early printing on Mallorca and, upstairs, a good collection of 20thC art, including Picasso, Miró (see **A-Z**) and the Sóller painter Juli Ramis (1909-90). See* **BUILDINGS 2**.

MUSEU MUNICIPAL DE POLLENÇA

Claustre de Santo Domingo, Pollença.
▓ 1000-1200 Tue., Thu. & Sun. ● Inexpensive.
Housed in a 17thC monastery, the museum displays prizewinning paintings and sculptures from the annual international art competition. See
EXCURSION 2.

MUSEU MONOGRÀFIC DE POLLENTIA c/ Sant Jaume 30,

Alcúdia. ▓ 0900-1300, 1700-2000 Tue.-Fri., 1000-1300 Sat. & Sun.
● Inexpensive.
*Displays important finds from the excavated sites of Urbs Pollentia, the Roman (see **A-Z**) name for Alcúdia. See* **EXCURSION 3**.

MUSEU ETNOLÒGIC DE MALLORCA

c/ Major 15, Muro.
▓ 1000-1400, 1600-1900 Tue.-Sat., 1000-1400 Sun. ● Inexpensive.
Museum devoted to traditional Mallorca life style, crafts and costume.

MUSEU REGIONAL D'ARTÀ

c/ Estrella 4, Artà.
▓ 1000-1200 Mon.-Fri. ● Free.
Archaeological collection of finds from local sites, including 2ndC BC bronzes. Also has temporary exhibitions of art. See **EXCURSION 3**.

TORRE DELS ENEGISTES

Ctra Calas de Mallorca s/n, Manacor.
▓ 0900-1300 Tue.-Thu. ● Inexpensive.
Archaeological museum in one of the remaining fortress towers containing prehistoric, Roman and Moorish finds. See **EXCURSION 3**.

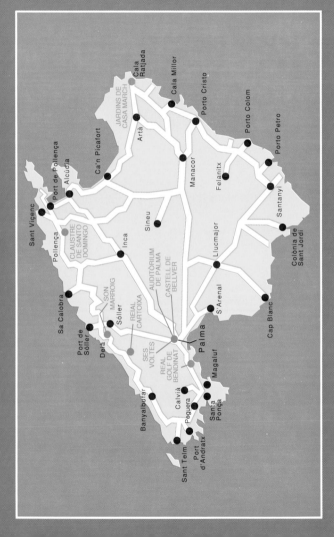

*A brochure giving full details of Mallorca's annual music festivals is available at tourist offices (see **Tourist Information**).*

AUDITÒRIUM DE PALMA Passeig Maritim 18.
▨ Performances usually at 2200.
Palma's main indoor venue for classical (and some jazz) concerts.

SES VOLTES Parc de la Mar, Palma.
▨ Performances start between 1900 & 2200.
Excellent outdoor venue for classical, rock and folk concerts.

CASTELL DE BELLVER Above Es Terreno, Palma.
▨ Performances usually at 2200 July & Aug. *Superb atmosphere and surroundings for summer series of classical concerts. See* **BUILDINGS 2**.

REAL GOLF DE BENDINAT Urb. Bendinat, Illetes.
▨ Performances at 2200 or 2300 Sat. (Aug.).
Annual classical music series, Concerts a l'Herba *(concerts on the grass).*

REIAL CARTOIXA (REAL CARTUJA) Valldemossa.
▨ Performances usually at 2200 Sun. (Aug.).
The annual Chopin piano festival (also works by other composers) attracts international soloists. See **BUILDINGS 2**.

SON MARROIG Deià. ▨ Performances usually at 2100 July-Sep.
Principal venue for Deià's annual international festival of classical music. See **BUILDINGS 2**.

CLAUSTRE DE SANTO DOMINGO Pollença.
▨ Performances usually at 2200 July & Aug.
Concerts in the elegant cloister during the international music festival at Pollença, founded by Philip Newman in 1962. See **EXCURSION 2**.

JARDINS DE CASA MARCH Cala Ratjada.
▨ Performances usually at 2200 July. *Extensive gardens and modern sculptures form the beautiful surroundings for summer concerts.*

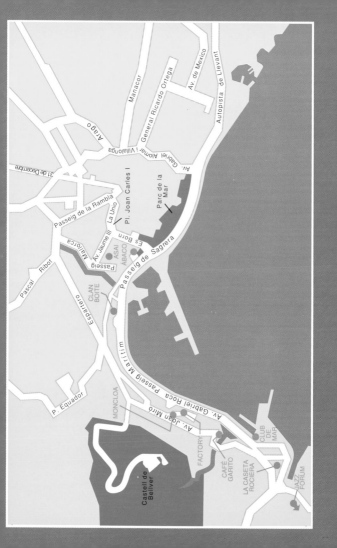

Palma

At night in central Palma, c/ Apuntadores is the liveliest street. Further out, the districts of Es Terreno and Es Jonquet are densely packed with late-night bars and discos. Many places are closed Sun.

CAFÉ GARITO Passeig Maritim, Darsena de Ca'n Barbara.
Café-bar with good atmosphere, live music and art exhibitions.

CLUB DE MAR Passeig Maritim (Club de Mar).
High-priced drinks in this music/dance bar. Favourite of international 'yachties' and Palma's wealthy class. Selective about clientele.

FACTORY Plaça Mediterráneo.
Palma's very young set gather until 0700 in this music bar which looks like an early-1900s factory.

ASAI Plaça Porta de Santa Catalina.
Central Palma's liveliest bar at weekends, particularly after 2400.

MONCLOA Plaça Gomila, Es Terreno.
Spanish and international music in this late-night rendezvous. Terrazzas overlook the square.

CLAN BOITE Plaça Vapor, Es Jonquet.
Elegant and luxurious disco/bar, now a favourite haunt of late-teens and early-twenties nightbirds.

ÁBACO c/ Sant Joan 1.
Go before or after dinner for exotic, very expensive cocktails among the huge displays of fruit and vegetables in this ultra-chic old palace.

LA CASETA ROCIERA Passeig Maritim, Porto Pi.
A good place to see flamenco and join the craze for dancing sevillanas.

JAZZ FORUM Avinguda Joan Miró 292, Cala Major.
The island's best venue for enjoying jazz. Go about 2400.

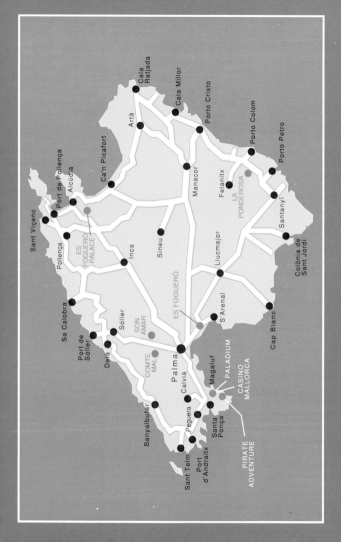

Dinner & Show

Most of the places listed below are destinations for organized excursions but individuals and families are also welcome.

ES FOGUERÓ Ctra Palma-Santanyí. End of motorway. Tel: 712699.
■ Dinner 2030, show 2200 Mon.-Sat. (summer), Wed.-Sat. (winter).
● Expensive.
Spanish dancing, traditional and contemporary, followed by a cabaret.

CASINO MALLORCA Urb. Sol de Mallorca, Magaluf, tel: 130000.
■ Gaming rooms 2000-0400, restaurant 2030-0130. ● Expensive.
Roulette, blackjack, craps, etc. Slot machines. Passport essential.

PALADIUM Casino Mallorca (see above). For reservations,
tel: 130000. ■ Dinner 2000, show 2200 Mon.-Sat. ● Expensive.
Spanish music and dance show followed by international 'spectacular'.

COMTE MAL Son Termens, Bunyola, tel: 610069.
■ Open 2030, dinner & show 2100 Mon., Wed., Fri. & Sat. ● Moderate.
Wenches serve a medieval banquet. Knights joust and frolic.

SON AMAR Ctra Palma-Sóller. 11 km from Palma. Tel: 753614.
■ 2015 Mon.-Sat. (summer), Wed. & Sat. (winter). ● Moderate.
Barbecue, folk dancing and top-of-the-bill entertainers of yesteryear.

PIRATE ADVENTURE Ctra La Porrasa, Magaluf, tel: 130411.
■ 2000-2400 summer. ● Moderate.
Pirates board a mock-up ship. Lots of fun, audience participation and prizes. Ends with dancing, and eating and drinking as much as you can.

ES FOGUERÓ PALACE Ctra Alcúdia-Sa Pobla, tel: 890285.
■ Dinner 2030, show 2230 May-Oct. ● Expensive.
Performances of Spanish dance, and cabaret acts.

LA PONDEROSA Ctra S'Horta, Felanitx.
■ 2000 Wed. (May-Sep.). ● Moderate.
'Western'-style barbecue and entertainment.

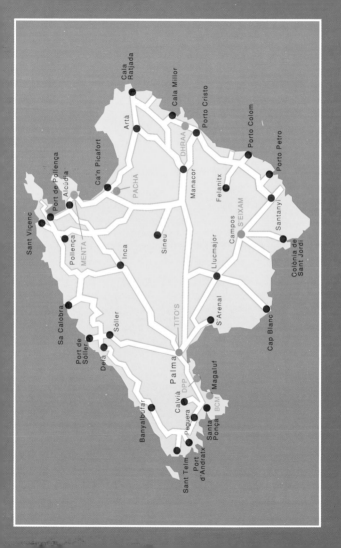

Discos

There's no shortage of these late-night venues in the resorts. Many hotels and apartment complexes have their own. See **NIGHTLIFE 1**.

BCM Avinguda S'Olivera, Magaluf.
Mallorca's most spectacular disco. Absolutely huge and decked out as a futuristic Roman temple! Latest sound, light and TARM laser equipment. Five video screens. Concerts by top international stars. Below, the Royale Nightclub is totally different – dance bands play nostalgic tunes and grupos rocieros accompany sevillanas. There's also a restaurant serving pizzas and international dishes.

TITO'S Entrance off Plaça Gomila & Passeig Maritim, Es Terreno, Palma.
Palma's top disco. Big place with good sound and light systems. Grand views of the bay. Live performances.

DHRAA Ctra Porto Cristo-Cala Millor.
Unusual, attractively designed nightspot. Dance indoors or under the stars. Good international music.

S'EIXAM Ctra Palma-Santanyí, Campos.
Currently one of the island's most popular discos. The design is Post-modern, the music Black-American.

MENTA Avinguda Tucán, Port d'Alcúdia.
This long-established disco with elegant interior and a reputation for playing the latest sounds continues to be popular. Round the corner is Mágica, with imaginative décor and live music.

PACHA Ctra de Santa Margalida, Ca'n Picafort.
Terrace, garden and pleasant disco for 1000 people. Mostly Spanish nightbirds. Nearby, the Rojo Disco is much more a foreigners' favourite.

DPP Port Portals, Portals Nous.
One of Mallorca's newest discos. Very expensive drinks for the very trendy and the island's young jetset.

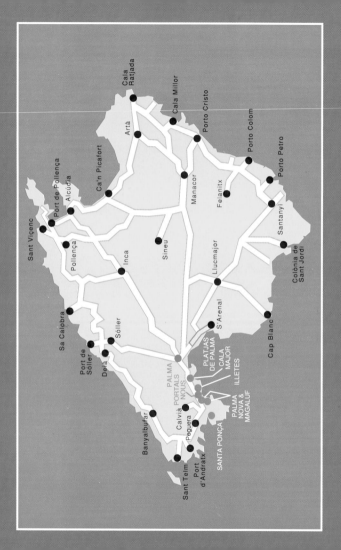

PLATJAS DE PALMA
Including Cala Gamba, Ca'n Pastilla, S'Arenal, Cala Blava.
Purpose-built resorts of high-rise accommodation, average eating places and many bars and discos along nearly 5 km of beach. See **A-Z**.

PALMA
Including Es Terreno, Son Vida.
The beach resorts along the bay of Palma are within easy reach of the city. Son Vida is a smart, inland urban district with excellent sports facilities. Es Terreno has lots of lively places for eating, drinking and nightlife.

CALA MAJOR TO PEGUERA
Along the scenic coast southwest of Palma there is a continuous ribbon development of modern resorts which operate all year. See **RESORTS 2**.

CALA MAJOR
Including Sant Agustí, Ca's Català.
Spain's royal family have their summer holiday home on the northern promontory of this cala. Long, sandy beach; good amenities. See **A-Z**.

ILLETES
With Portals Nous, this resort is regarded as more up-market than others along this coast. It has the best facilities but gets crowded. See **A-Z**.

PORTALS NOUS
Including Costa de Bendinat, Costa d'en Blanes.
Has a narrow strip of sandy beach as well as rocky areas with coves of shingle or sand beaches. Very up-market shops, restaurants and nightlife.

PALMA NOVA & MAGALUF
Bustling and brash, these two resorts epitomize the mass tourism for which Mallorca is best known. Two wide bays; sandy beaches. See **A-Z**.

SANTA PONÇA
Set on the scoop of a bay backed by low hills, this resort has rapidly acquired the mini-Miami look but the pace is less hectic. See **A-Z**.

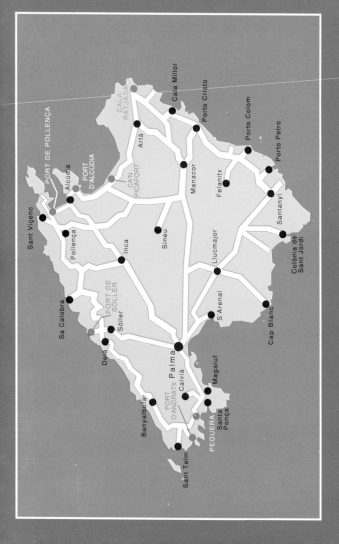

PEGUERA

Some old buildings line the seafront of this relatively new, quite compact resort surrounded by pine woods. The busy Palma-Andratx road separates the heart of the resort from its four good, sandy beaches. See A-Z.

PORT D'ANDRATX

Including Camp de Mar, Sant Telm.
The character of this small fishing village has not yet been lost, though it is now a favourite with the yachting fraternity and has a growing number of tourist facilities. There are simple bars, cafés and restaurants. See A-Z.

PORT DE SÓLLER

A picturesque port with a palm-fringed beach of sand and shingle, and simple eating and drinking places. See EXCURSION 4, A-Z.

PORT DE POLLENÇA

Including Cala Sant Viçenc, Formentor.
From tiny hostals and purpose-built 'package' hotels to the grandness of the famous Hotel Formentor, there's a wide choice of places to stay in an area that attracts a mix of ages and nationalities. See EXCURSION 2, A-Z.

PORT D'ALCÚDIA

Including Platjas de Mallorca.
Most of the new developments lie to the east of the old harbour and for about 4 km line the curve of the bay and the beach of white sand. Like most of the resorts along to Cala Ratjada, Port d'Alcúdia is mainly popular with Germans. See EXCURSION 3, A-Z.

CA'N PICAFORT

Although unimaginatively designed, this modern resort along the middle of Alcúdia bay caters especially well for families. See EXCURSION 3, A-Z.

CALA RATJADA

Including Cala de Sa Font, Cala Agulla.
Restrained development on this beautiful coast means that Cala Ratjada retains the charm of an active fishing port. See EXCURSION 3, A-Z.

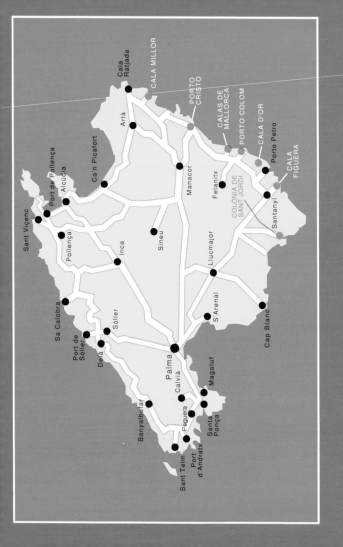

CALA MILLOR
Including Cala Bona, Costa dels Pins, Platja de Canyamel.
High-rise blocks of hotels, apartments and other amenities catering for a mass market are packed along a 1.5 km stretch of fine sand beach which is well serviced. The summer scene here can be very hectic. See **A-Z**.

PORTO CRISTO
Inc. S'Illot, Cala Moreia, Sa Coma, Porto Cristo Novo, Cala Estany.
A small-scale resort, though day-trippers to the caves of Drac and Hams (see **CAVES**) *make the otherwise charming and picturesque village very crowded during the high season. See* **A-Z**.

CALAS DE MALLORCA
From Cala Magrana to Cala Murada.
Purpose-built holiday complex of big hotels and apartments on a barren headland. There are a number of sandy coves backed by cliffs.

PORTO COLOM
Including Cala Marsal.
Bright little houses line the waterfront of this active fishing village. Its large protected bay has few beaches but is perfect for water sports. It is popular with the islanders and mainland Spaniards.

CALA D'OR
Including Porto Petro.
One of the island's larger new resorts and one of its most attractive. Set round pine-fringed coves with small sandy beaches. See **A-Z**.

CALA FIGUERA
Including Cala Santanyí, Cala Llombards.
The hotels and apartments being built here won't encroach on the narrow inlet which this picturesque and busy fishing village hugs. To the south are some of the island's loveliest unspoilt coves. See **A-Z**.

COLÒNIA DE SANT JORDI
Small village and port. Low-key but developing. See **A-Z**.

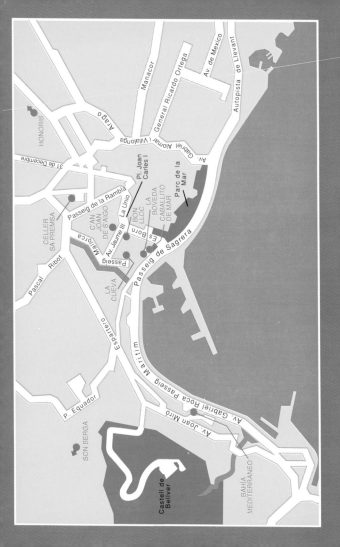

BAHÍA MEDITERRANEO Passeig Maritim 33, tel: 458877.
● Expensive.
Very elegant dining. Well-chosen international dishes perfectly prepared and presented. Turbot in champagne is a speciality.

HONORIS Ctra Vella (Vieja) Bunyola 76, tel: 203212.
● Moderate (lunch), Expensive (dinner).
Smart service in elegant rooms or lovely garden. Different evening menu presents modern Mediterranean cuisine. Highly recommended.

SON BERGA Ctra de Palma, Génova, tel: 433869. ● Moderate.
Good, traditional fare in converted farm buildings.

CABALLITO DE MAR Passeig de Sagrera 5, tel: 721074.
● Moderate.
*Fish, seafood specialities. Terrace views of La Llotja (see **BUILDINGS 1**).*

LA CUEVA c/ Apuntadores 5. ■ 2030-0030. ● Moderate.
*Excellent tapas (see **Food**). Arrive early if you want a table.*

LA BOVEDA c/ de la Boteria 3, tel: 714863.
■ 1330-1600, 2030-0030 Mon.-Sat. ● Inexpensive.
Elegant turn-of-the-century building where full meals or snacks are served. Very popular with Mallorquins.

CELLER SA PREMSA Plaça Bisbe Berenguer de Palou 8,
tel: 723629. ■ Closed Sat. & Sun. ● Inexpensive.
Big and usually bustling with locals and tourists. Basic Mallorcan fare.

C'AN JOAN DE S'AIGO c/ Santa Maria del Sepulchre.
■ 0900-2100. ● Inexpensive.
*Try the chocolate ensaimada (see **Food**). Almond ice cream a speciality.*

BON LLOC c/ Sant Feliu 7, tel: 718617.
■ 1300-1600 Tue.-Sat., 2030-2300 Fri. ● Inexpensive.
Tasty vegetarian and vegan cooking.

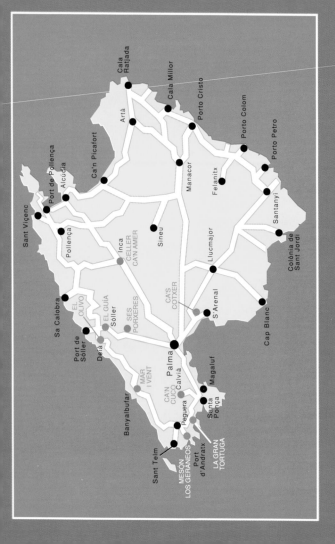

EL OLIVO Hotel La Residencia, Deià, tel: 639392.
■ Expensive.
Gourmet restaurant at one of the island's most famous hotels.

CA'S COTXER Ctra de S'Arenal 31, Les Meravelles, Platja de Palma, tel: 262049. ● Moderate.
Busy but attentive. Extensive and creative menu.

LA GRAN TORTUGA Ctra Cala Fornells, Peguera, tel: 686023.
■ Closed Mon. Reservations advisable. ● Moderate.
Stylish décor and service. Terrace and swimming pool. Serves an international menu.

MESÓN LOS GERÁNEOS Avinguda Mateo Bosch 4, Port d'Andratx, tel: 673642. ● Moderate.
Mallorcan décor and cooking. List of island and Spanish wines.

MAR I VENT c/ Primo de Riviera 57, Banyalbufar, tel: 618000.
■ 1800-2100. ● Moderate.
Memorable home cooking in this delightful family-run hotel.

SES PORXERES Ctra Palma-Sóller, Jardins de Alfabia, tel: 613762.
■ Closed Sun. evening, Mon. & Aug. ● Moderate.
Delicious Catalan cooking in a tastefully converted barn.

CA'N CUCO Avinguda de Palma 14, Calvià, tel: 670083.
■ Closed Mon., & lunch July & Aug. ● Inexpensive.
Plain and simple. Local favourite for good-value Mallorcan food.

EL GUÍA c/ Castanyer 1, Sóller, tel: 613762.
● Inexpensive.
Dining room of family-run hotel serves big helpings of Mallorcan food.

CELLER CA'N AMER c/ Bruy 7, Inca, tel: 501261.
■ Closed Sat. evening & Sun. ● Inexpensive.
Typical of the town's famous cellers.

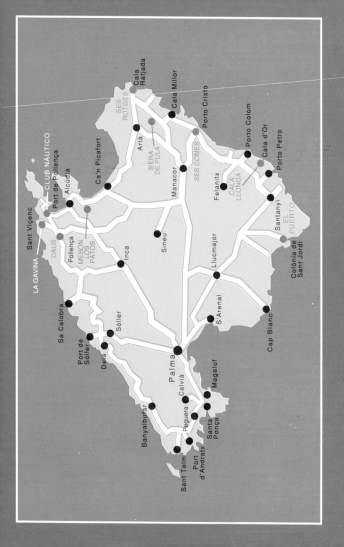

North & East

MESÓN LOS PATOS Ctra Sa Pobla-Alcúdia, Port d'Alcúdia.
■ Closed Tue. ● Expensive.
Large restaurant specializing in extremely high quality, traditional Mallorcan cooking. Terrace and gardens, swimming pool, videos, etc.

LA GAVINA c/ Temporal s/n, Cala Sant Viçenc, tel: 530155.
● Moderate.
High standard of cuisine in a 1930s setting. Seafood specialities.

DAUS c/ Calvari 10, Pollença, tel: 532867. ■ Closed Tue. ● Moderate.
Specializes in modern versions of old Mallorcan recipes.

CLUB NÁUTICO Moll Vell s/n, Port de Pollença, tel: 531648.
● Moderate.
Fresh fish and shellfish on the wharf. Terrace with excellent views.

SES ROTGES c/ Rafael Blanes 21, Cala Ratjada, tel: 563108.
■ Closed lunch Nov.-Mar. ● Moderate.
Large old house with tower, now an elegant hotel and restaurant. Enjoys high reputation for its French and local cuisine. Tables also in courtyard.

S'ERA DE PULA Ctra Son Servera-Capdepera, Son Servera,
tel: 567940. ■ 1220-1530, 1800-2400 Tue.-Sun. ● Moderate.
Converted farmhouse. Fresh fish is served depending on the market.

CALA LLONGA Porto Cari i Apartamentos s/n, Cala d'Or,
tel: 658036. ● Moderate.
Modern and spacious. Seafood specialist but good meat selection too.

EL PUERTO c/ Puerto 13, Colònia de Sant Jordi, tel: 656047.
● Moderate.
Superb paellas and fresh fish dishes for locals and tourists.

SES COMES Avinguda dels Pins 24, Porto Cristo, tel: 821254.
■ Closed Mon. ● Inexpensive.
Fish and seafood served in this unpretentious eatery on outskirts of town.

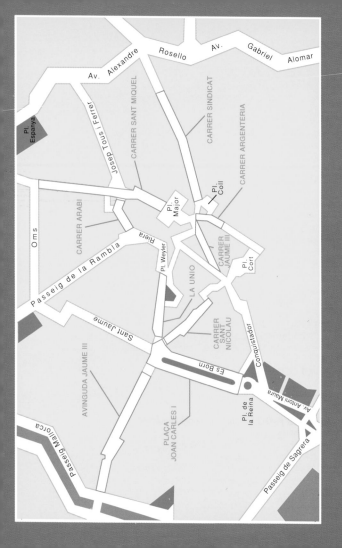

AVINGUDA JAUME III
The town's largest shopping street, with all types of quality retailers and a branch of Galerías Preciados, Mallorca's only department store.

PLAÇA JOAN CARLES I
For clothing, there is a branch of the C&A chain. Good shops for pearls, leather and suede, and jewellery. Down Es Born you'll find espadrilles, embroidery, and perfume shops.

CARRER SANT NICOLAU
Narrow streets in one of Palma's old quarters, delightful for browsing and wandering. Good charcuterie, sweets, espadrilles, wines and spirits.

CARRER JAUME III
Modern designer clothes shops, as well as old-fashioned speciality shops. Fascinating fans and umbrellas at Segura Arrecio. Across the street is a good place for gloves and haberdashery.

CARRER ARGENTERIA
Almost every shop is a jeweller, eager to sell old and modern pieces.

CARRER SINDICAT
Many low-priced bazaars. Exotic smells in spice shops where saffron is a good buy. Shoes and woven straw items too.

CARRER SANT MIQUEL
Old books and prints at Librería Ripoll. Also shoes, embroidery work, charcuterie, clothes, woven straw goods, ceramics and glass.

CARRER ARABI
Antique shops can be found here and in nearby streets.

LA UNIO
Shoes, sports gear, toys, Lladró porcelain and pastries. Round the corner in Plaça Weyler is the pretty front of Forn d'es Teatre (see SHOPPING 2). Elsewhere, you can buy iron and steel Toledo ware.

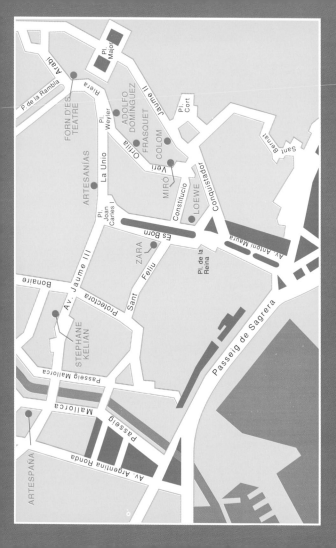

ADOLFO DOMÍNGUEZ
Plaça del Mercat 13.
Stylish clothes by Spain's most famous designer in the equally stylish Modernista building, Edifici Casasayas (see BUILDINGS 1, **Modernista**).

LOEWE Es Born 2.
High-quality leather and suede clothes, accessories and perfume.

ZARA Es Born 25.
Big store selling young-style fashionable clothes at moderate prices.

STEPHANE KELIAN Avinguda Jaume III 16.
Fashionable footwear by acclaimed designers.

MIRÓ Plaça Rosari 11.
Wide range of jewellery. Smart shop with attentive service.

ARTESPAÑA Passeig Mallorca 17.
Selection of some of the best design and craft items from all over Spain.

FORN D'ES TEATRE
Plaça Weyler 11.
Prettily painted old shopfront with, inside, a mouthwatering selection of ensaimadas (see **Food***), cakes and pastries.*

ARTESANÍAS La Unio 13.
A vast selection of traditional Spanish ceramics, pottery and glass.

COLOM c/ Santo Domingo 5.
Epicurean delights, groceries, fresh fish and vegetables.

FRASQUET c/ Orfila 4.
Chocolates and other sweets. Nice ideas for take-home gifts.

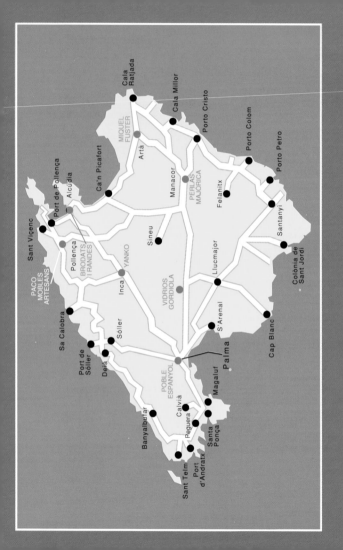

POBLE ESPANYOL

c/ Poble Espanyol 39, Palma.

■ 1000-1800 Mon.-Sat.

See crafts, including pottery, glass-blowing, leatherwork and jewellery, before browsing in the shops. See **BUILDINGS 1**.

PERLAS MAJÓRICA

Avinguda Majorca 48, Manacor.

■ 0900-1300, 1500-1800 Mon.-Fri., 0900-1300 Sat.

Tour of the factory making famous artificial pearls, followed by the tempting shop. See **EXCURSION 3**.

YANKO

Ctra Palma-Alcúdia, Inca.

One of several leatherworks for which the town is famous. Prices are lower than in the shops.

PACO MOBLES ARTESANS

Rotonda de Pollença (roundabout), Pollença.

Large shop and display galleries of crafts, including ceramics, basket-work and furniture.

BRODATS I RANDES

Carrer d'en Serra 17b, Alcúdia.

Beautiful traditional embroideries and textiles.

MIQUEL FUSTER

c/ Pep Not 16, Artà.

A shop selling traditional woven straw and grasswork items.

VIDRIOS GORDIOLA

Ctra Palma-Manacor, Algaida.

Demonstrations of glass-blowing, plus a shop and a small museum.

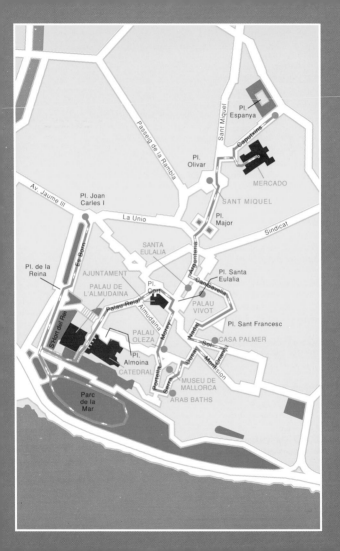

East of Es Born

Duration: 2 hr 45 min, excluding visits.

Begin at Plaça Espanya. Note the statue of Jaume I (see **A-Z**). Go south-west into c/ dels Caputxins towards Plaça Olivar. Exit into c/ Sant Miquel and turn left. There are some good shops here. Sant Miquel church has an impressive altar. Pass into the attractive Plaça Major, where you'll find shops, bars, an underground bazaar and a craft market. Continue into Plaça Marqués de Palmer and bear left into c/ Argenteria, with its many jewellers. Turn left into c/ Can Savella to see Palau Vivot. The second right leads to Plaça Sant Francesc. Visit the church and cloister (see **BUILDINGS 1**) and see the statue of Junipero Serra (see **A-Z**) and an American Indian child. Turn into c/ Pare Nadal and left into c/ del Sol to see the solid Casa Palmer (1556) with its Renaissance decoration and upper gallery, a copy of La Llotja's (see **BUILDINGS 1**). Along these narrow streets you'll see more old palaces. Peek into their patios. Turn right on c/ Criança, right again on c/ Montision, left along c/ Dusai and across to c/ Serra and the Arab baths (No. 7) and small garden (see **Moors**). Continue round into c/ Portella, heart of the Call, once the Jewish district near the old city walls. The Museu de Mallorca is at No. 5 (see **MUSEUMS 1**). Continue into c/ Morey and look into the Palau Oleza's impressive patio. Up on the left across c/ Almudaina, notice an arch from the Arab walls. Enter Plaça Santa Eulalia, dominated by its church. It has fine external carvings and a high-vaulted Gothic nave. The square is a charming, shady place to take refreshment. Leave by c/ Cadena into Plaça Cort with the handsome Ajuntament (see **BUILDINGS 1**). Go left into c/ Palau Reial. On the left in c/ Almudaina are Casa Oleo (No. 4), with notable patio and staircase, and Casa Vilallonga (No. 13), with small Plateresque windows. Continue to Plaça Almoina, and admire the Catedral and Palau de l'Almudaina (see **BUILDINGS 1**). On the south side of Plaça Almoina, go down the steps to a terrace for panoramas across the bay. Steps to the right lead to the bronze statue of a *foner* (see **A-Z**) with his sling. Detour to the Parc de la Mar, reclaimed from the sea and opened in 1984, with abstract forms by Alfaro and a mural by Miró (see **A-Z**). Return to the centre via the S'Hort del Rei gardens, with their fountains and cypress trees, through Plaça de la Reina up the eastern side of Es Born, which has interesting shops, and finish at Plaça Joan Carles I.

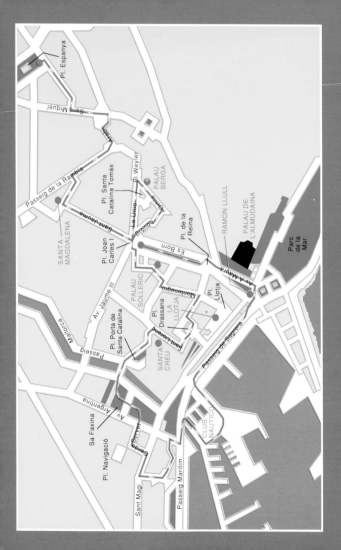

West of Es Born

Duration: 2 hr 45 min.

Begin at Plaça Joan Carles I. Go down the centre of Es Born and along Avinguda Antoni Maura to the statue of Ramon Llull (see **A-Z**) at the end. On the left is the Palau de l'Almudaina's Gothic gallery (see **BUILDINGS 1**). Turn right into Passeig de Sagrera, with a number of seafood restaurants. Go right into Plaça Llotja and stop to admire the grand Gothic building (see **BUILDINGS 1**). Continue along Passeig de Sagrera then left across Passeig Maritim to reach the fishing boat harbour, usually bustling with lots of local colour. Stroll along to the contrasting scene of the yacht-filled Club Náutico. Cross Passeig Maritim again and go left across Avinguda Argentina and up some steps into the district of Es Jonquet with its preserved windmills (see **A-Z**), many bars and nightspots. Go on to Plaça Vapor, a lively neighbourhood focal point, then right on c/ Sant Magi, and left on c/ Cerda to Plaça Navigació and its fresh food market. Turn right into c/ Servet and cross Avinguda Argentina again to Sa Faxina memorial garden. Turn right across the bridge over the Torrent de Riera (dry in summer). Go through Plaça Porta de Santa Catalina. Asai (see **NIGHTLIFE 1**) is on the left. Note the Baroque portico of Santa Creu church. Turn right into old, narrow (and sometimes smelly) c/ Sant Llorenç, then left and through Plaça Drassana, a working-class gathering place, to c/ Apuntadores. This is a lively street with many bars and varied eating places. Go left into c/ Montenegro. Admire the distinctive courtyard at No. 2. Turn right into c/ Gaieta and see Palau Solleric with an elegantly proportioned patio and gallery, one of Palma's finest. To the right, an alley leads to Plaça Joan Carles I. For just a taste of Palma's shopping delights, cross over to c/ Brondo, leading to c/ Sant Nicolau and go left along c/ Orfila to Plaça Santa Catalina Tomás. Note the imposing façade of Palau Berga (law courts). Turn left along c/ Unio past Casa Balaguer, and return to Plaça Joan Carles I. Go right into c/ Sant Jaume, an evocative street. Note the Hostal Born's courtyard (No. 3) and art galleries (Nos 6 and 15). Bar Angel (No. 7) is a pleasant spot to have a drink. Turn right by Santa Magdalena church to reach Passeig de La Rambla. Turn right down this shaded avenue with its flower stalls and left at c/ Pols to reach c/ Arabi with its antique shops. Turn left again into c/ Sant Miquel and right through Plaça Olivar. Finish at Plaça Espanya.

Alcúdia: Close to the resorts of Alcúdia bay, this was once the Roman city of Pollentia, and the sites of the forum, theatre and houses have been excavated. Sections of the medieval walls and several of the gates to the town still remain and behind them are narrow streets with some fine buildings. See **EXCURSION 3**.

Andratx: A pleasant village set in a valley of farmland and orchard gardens. Its Wed. market is a focus for visitors to the resorts in the southwestern tip of the island.

Anglada i Camarasa, Hermen (1872-1959): A Modernista (see **A-Z**) painter from Barcelona who spent his latter years at Port de Pollença. Like most artists of his generation, he moved to Paris at the beginning of the century. In style and subject matter he is comparable with other artists of Symbolist and Art Nouveau movements throughout Europe. An important collection of his work opens at the Fundació La Caixa, Palma in 1993 (see **MUSEUMS 1**).

Artà: The sanctuary of Sant Salvador dominates this small town of steep and narrow streets. Nearby are the Bronze-Age *talaiots* of Ses Païsses, while the caves of Artà are 9 km southeast. See **EXCURSION 3**.

Banyalbufar: A village in an extremely attractive setting of wide terraces and gnarled old olive trees dating from Moorish times. It was once protected by a series of watchtowers, including the Talaia de Ses Animas (see **Talaias**) whose mirador has good views.

Binissalem: The main town for the island's wine production, Binissalem's obvious attractions are its bodegas and shops where the product can be tasted and bought. Throughout the summer there are folk dancing displays in the square.

Bronze Age: The *poblado* of Capicorp Vell, south of Llucmajor, is the island's best-preserved Bronze-Age settlement. There are excavated houses, tunnels and two *talaiots* (see **A-Z**). Ask at the house opposite to gain entry. Near Artà are Ses Païsses (see **EXCURSION 3**), remains of another settlement, and the *talaiots* of Sa Canova. Near Son Baul are to be found the remains of the 7thC BC necropolis of Son Real. See **EXCURSION 3**.

Bullfighting: Its aficionados regard the performance as an art form, a ritualized ballet in which the lurking danger to the man heightens the intensity. The fate of the *toro* is always the same. Palma's Plaça de Toros Monumental has corridas on summer Sun. Coach excursions run from most resorts. Bullrings at Inca, Muro and Alcúdia are used less frequently. Children under 15 are not admitted.

Cala Agulla: See **BEACHES**, Cala Ratjada.

Cala Blava: See Platjas de Palma.

Cala Bona: See Cala Millor.

Cala de Sa Font: See Cala Ratjada.

Cala d'Or

Cala d'Or: This large, new and attractive resort is especially popular with Scandinavian tourists. Most of its buildings successfully blend modern and traditional design. The range of accommodation, sports and entertainments is comprehensive and the resort caters well for younger people and active families. It also has the east coast's best selection of shops, restaurants and nightspots. In the pretty fishing port of Porto Petro there's a contrasting choice of simpler accommodation and places to eat. Nearby Cala Mondragó (see **BEACHES**) has a large, inviting beach of fine sand. See **RESORTS 3**.

Cala Estany: See **Porto Cristo**.

Cala Figuera: Facilities are mainly limited to a few modest places to stay and eat but the fishing village itself retains its traditional charm. Further to the south are some of the island's loveliest unspoilt coves. Calas Santanyí and Llombards have facilities, though others have none and can only be reached by foot or boat. See **RESORTS 3**.

Cala Gamba: See **RESORTS 1**.

Cala Major: The large establishments purpose-built for the package holiday industry predominate along this stretch of coastline to the southwest of Palma. However, accommodation is still available in hotels and apartments of all classes and in villas, chalets and bunga-lows. The majority of shops, bars, eating places and nightlife venues cater largely for young foreign holiday-makers who don't want to spend too much. Good facilities for healthy fun are available at numerous sports clubs, pleasure marinas and water-sports centres. Transport between resorts is easy by road or on boat excursions. Cala Major includes the resorts of Sant Agustí and Ca's Català. See **RESORTS 1**.

Cala Marsal: See **RESORTS 3**.

Cala Millor: A highly-developed tourist resort area. In high season the pace here can be as hectic as that in the big resorts around Palma bay. It is much quieter at the Cala Bona end, where there's a small

fishing port with water sports and three artificial coves. Costa dels Pins is an exclusive development with luxury villas, golf courses and top-class hotels. Platja de Canyamel, lined with pines and protected by cliffs, is being developed with discretion. See **RESORTS 3**.

Cala Moreia: See **Porto Cristo**.

Cala Ratjada: Many of the villas, hotels and restaurants have idyllic settings along this attractive stretch of coastline and modern developments have been well controlled. There are all types of beaches: shingle and rocks of the central bathing area; the sand and rocks of Platja Son Moll; rocky Cala Çat; Cala Agulla (see **BEACHES**); and Cala de Sa Font's two tiny coves of fine, soft sand. The Jardins Casa March are beautiful and extensive gardens containing modern sculptures by Henry Moore and others. To visit them, contact the local tourist office, tel: 563033. See **EXCURSION 3**, **RESORTS 2**.

Cala Sant Vicenç: See **Port de Pollença**.

Cala Santanyí: See **Cala Figuera**.

Calas de Mallorca

Calas de Mallorca: See RESORTS 3.

Calvià: Set on a little hill and approached through attractive scenery, Calvià is the main administrative centre and market town for the south-west. Its parish church dates originally from the 13thC.

Camp de Mar: See Port d'Andratx.

Ca'n Pastilla: See Platjas de Palma.

Ca'n Picafort: This resort, although well-supplied with amenities, is not the most attractive of the island's recent developments. The ser-viced main beach is long and narrow with white sand and occasional rocks. Son Bauló beach has coarser sand, dunes and some shade. The more tranquil Platjas de Muro (see **BEACHES**) have a layer of small shells on soft sand. Excursions include trips in glass-bottomed boats to a tiny island with prehistoric remains. See **EXCURSION 3, RESORTS 2**.

Capdepera: A picturesque hill town near the resort of Cala Ratjada on the road to Artà. On its hill top is a ruined castle (open access; free) built in the reign of the 14thC King Sanxo of Mallorca, with a small ora-tory and good views from the battlements.See **EXCURSION 3**.

Ca's Català: See Cala Major.

Catedral, Palma: Construction of Palma's impressive Gothic cathe-dral began in 1230, immediately after the Christian conquest of the island on the site of the main mosque, and continued until 1587. The west façade was largely rebuilt after an earthquake in 1851 but the beautiful south or Mirador doorway begun in 1389 survives. The cathe-dral is entered through the chapterhouses containing treasures, includ-ing the portable altarpiece brought by Jaume I in 1229, 14th-16thC paintings and massive Baroque silver candlesticks. The main nave is well lit by the rose windows of the apse. Above the high altar is the unusual canopy by Gaudí (see **Modernista**) and, behind it, 14thC choir stalls by Camprodón. To the left of the chancel is a magnificent pulpit of 1531 by Juan de Salas and, in the north aisle, the vast 17thC Corpus Christi altarpiece. Behind the choir are the tombs of Mallorcan kings Jaume II and III. See **BUILDINGS 1**.

Caves: *Coves* in Mallorquin, *cuevas* in Castilian. There are many marvellous limestone caves on the island. Some are said to have been the hide-outs of Mallorca's notorious pirates and smugglers down the centuries. Surprisingly, not all have been explored and only the most spectacular have been developed as tourist attractions. See **CAVES**.

Chopin, Frédéric (1810-49): In the winter of 1838-39 the Polish composer rented some of the cells recently vacated by the monks of Valldemossa's Carthusian monastery (see **BUILDINGS 2**), where he spent about three months with the French author George Sand (Aurora Dupin) and her two children. As she recorded in her book, *Winter in Mallorca*, they had a rather miserable time, liking very little of what they found. Chopin's stay is commemorated by the annual international piano festival (see **MUSIC**).

Colònia de Sant Jordi: A small and still relatively undeveloped resort with a harbour and restaurants. Nearby are the beaches of Es Trenc (see **BEACHES**), Ses Covetes and Sa Ràpita, and there are boat excursions to tiny Cabrera island. To the north are the hot springs of Banyas de Sant Joan and a spa hotel. The resort is convenient for birdwatchers visiting the salt flats of Salines de Llevant (see **Bird-watching**). See **RESORTS 3**.

Costa de Bendinat: See **RESORTS 1**.

Costa dels Pins: See **Cala Millor**.

Costa d'en Blanes: See **RESORTS 1**.

Deià: A picturesque village of narrow, cobbled streets and houses with flower-decked walls, where the English writer Robert Graves (1905-85) settled. It is now home to a thriving but exclusive artistic set. Of interest are the small archaeological museum (0930-1400 Mon.-Sat.), a series of tiled roadside altars marking stations of the Cross, and the famous hotel, La Residencia, which often has art exhibitions open to the public. Nearby is Son Marroig (see **BUILDINGS** 2), home of Archduke Ludwig Salvator (see **A-Z**).

Els Blavets: Named after their blue cassocks, these choirboys of the famous choir school, the Escolana de Lluc (established in 1531), sing at 1115 every day during morning Mass at the Monasterio de Lluc (see **BUILDINGS** 2).

Estellencs: An attractive village on the west coast with steep streets and pretty houses set in a landscape of terraces with orchards.

Es Terreno: See **RESORTS** 1.

Felanitx: One of the wine-making towns, Felanitx is also a centre for ceramic and enamel crafts. Nearby are the sanctuary of Sant Salvador and Santueri castle.

Foners: *Honderos* in Castilian. The islanders traditionally fought with stones and slings. The deadly accuracy of the *foners* became famous from the 3rd C BC, when they fought as mercenaries with the armies of Carthage. They successfully repelled Roman (see **A-Z**) invasions of the island but were eventually defeated in 123 BC. A modern statue of a *foner* is in Avinguda Antoni Maura in Palma (see **WALK** 1).

Formentor: See **BEACHES, EXCURSION** 2, **RESORTS** 2, **Port de Pollença**.

Illetes: Wooded hillsides and rocky promontories separate three coves with gently sloping beaches of fine sand. See **RESORTS** 1.

Inca: With few pretensions to being pretty, the island's third-largest town attracts many tourists to browse and buy at its leatherwork factories and shops. Its traditional eating places, *cellers*, serve delicious food, and *galletes d'oli* or *d'Inca* (Inca biscuits) are also worth trying.

Formentor

Jardins de Alfabia: Beautiful gardens laid out in Moorish style, just off the Palma–Sóller road. They include cool pools and refreshing fountains, while exotic trees provide welcome shade. The house contains an interesting 16thC chair with relief figures of Jaume IV, last of the Mallorcan kings, and his sister. See **BUILDINGS 2, EXCURSION 1**.

Jaume I (1207-76): Jaume I, king of Aragon and Catalunya, who routed the Moors (see **A-Z**) on Mallorca in 1229, became known as El Conqueridor (the Conqueror). His principal aim was to stop Mallorca being used as a base by pirates who severely disrupted trade between Catalunya and the rest of the Mediterranean. His son, Jaume II, became the first king of the short-lived Mallorcan dynasty. With Jaume II a Golden Age began: agriculture was improved and the island's fleet and foreign trade were expanded. Artists and writers had the king's patronage. Prosperity continued under Sanxo I, who reigned 1311-24, and his nephew Jaume III. In 1343, Pedro IV of Aragon deposed Jaume III and re-united Mallorca with Aragon. Jaume III was killed at the Battle of Llucmayor in 1349.

Juan Carlos I (1938-): Known as Joan Carles I in Mallorca, the king of Spain is a grandson of Spain's last monarch. Franco had named Juan Carlos to be his successor as head of state and when the dictator died in 1975 he was proclaimed king. The royal family take their summer holiday at the Marivent palace near Cala Major, where members of Europe's other royal houses are frequent guests.

La Granja: Northwest of Palma on the PM 110, 2 km from the village of Esporles, is La Granja, the beautiful country house estate of the Fortuny family and now a popular heritage centre of Mallorquin folk life. Islanders dressed in local costume demonstrate traditional crafts and customs from farming to spinning and baking. In the grounds are a spectacular natural fountain and displays of folk dancing and village games. See **BUILDINGS 2**.

Llauds: Looking like lifeboats of ocean liners, Mallorca's typical fishing boats are brightly-coloured open craft measuring 6-12 m.

Llull, Ramon (1233-1314): The Blessed Ramon Llull is credited with the revival of monastic and hermitic life on the island. The son of a Catalan nobleman who had fought in the Christian reconquest of Mallorca, he grew up to be a dissolute courtier. Later, he repented his earlier life and withdrew to Mount Randa, where he led the life of a hermit for a time. He also travelled widely, gaining an international reputation, and with the help of King Jaume II founded a school of Oriental studies on Mallorca. His poems, novels, and essays on theology and philosophy were written in Catalan, Provençal, Latin or Arabic. His last missionary journey was to Algiers where he suffered martyrdom by stoning.

Magaluf: See **Palma Nova & Magaluf**.

Manacor: Mallorca's second town is a busy place, servicing the east coast resorts. Its attractions include an archaeological museum (see **MUSEUMS 2**), the artificial pearls factory (see **SHOPPING 3**) and shops selling local pottery and olivewood items. See **EXCURSION 3**.

Miró, Joan (1893-1983): One of the most important artists of this century. He was born in Barcelona and moved to Paris in the 1920s, where he joined the Surrealist group and moved towards abstract compositions using bright colours. As well as paintings, his work included sculpture, ceramics and prints. He moved to Mallorca in 1940 and in his studios at Cala Major he revived the medieval practice of large artists' workshops where the master oversaw all the works produced. The Fundació Pilar i Joan Miró opens his studios to the public from the end of 1992 (see **MUSEUMS 1**).

Modernista: A movement in architecture, design and painting principally associated with Barcelona and Catalunya around the turn of the century, and similar to Art Nouveau elsewhere in Europe. Its most famous exponent was Antoni Gaudí (1852-1926). The painter Anglada i Camarasa (see **A-Z**) settled on Mallorca and there are also a number of important Modernista buildings on the island. In Palma, these include the Parlament Balear (see **BUILDINGS 1**), originally the building of the Círculo Mallorquín, with a façade by Miquel Madorell of 1913, and the twin buildings Edifici Casasayas and Pensió Menorquina (see **BUILDINGS 1**) by Francesc Roca and Guillem Reynés of 1908-11. The canopy over the main altar of Palma cathedral (see **BUILDINGS 1**, **A-Z**) was designed by Gaudí. In Sóller, the façade of the parish church of Sant Bartomeu and the Banco Sóller (see **EXCURSION 4**) are both by Joan Rubió i Bellver, a pupil of Gaudí, and date from 1904-13. See **MUSEUMS 1**.

Moors: The collective word describing Arab, Berber and other Muslims who invaded mainland Spain from North Africa in AD 711 and estab-lished their capital at Córdoba. They raided Mallorca continuously but a series of treaties kept them from domination of the island until 902. Christians who paid their taxes went unmolested and the island benefit-ed from the advanced culture and techniques of irrigation and agricul-ture the Moors brought. Following the collapse of the caliphate of Córdoba early in the 11thC, Mallorca came under the rule of walis, minor kings who treated the islanders harshly. They were replaced by a new wave of North Africans, the Almoravides, who allowed the remain-ing Christians to follow their religion and advanced the island's agricul-ture and trade. Persecution started again with the arrival in 1203 of the fanatical Almohades. On 31 Dec. 1229 King Jaume I (see **A-Z**) and his Catalan army breached the walls of Medina Mayurka (Palma) and cap-tured its ruler, Abu Yahya. Surprisingly little remains of Moorish architec-ture. Palma preserves the island's only Arab baths at c/ Serra (see **WALK 1**) (0900-2000 summer, 0930-1830 winter; Inexpensive). Probably dating from the 10thC, they contain a domed caldarium with slender columns. At the Palau de l'Almudaina (see **BUILDINGS 1**) the horseshoe arch typical of Islamic architecture is still discernible despite later alterations. Elsewhere on the island are a number of Moorish castles, among them Castell d'Alaró (see **EXCURSION 1**) and the impressive Castell del Rei (a 1.5 hr walk from Ternelles, near Pollença; access Sat. am only).

Mountains: The chain rising steeply above the western and north-western coastline, from Andratx to Formentor, creates the island's most spectacular scenery of barren crags, pine-covered slopes and verdant valleys. It hides small villages, tiny coves, fishing hamlets and stone-built

Formentor

terraces where olive, almond and citrus trees grow. Within a short distance the scene can change from barren and dramatic to quaint and picturesque. Often covered in mist, Puig Mayor rises to 1443 m; south across the Sóller valley is Puig Teix (1062 m); looming above Estellencs and Galilea there's Puig Galatza (1026 m). On the southern edge of the central plain, Puig Randa stands proudly at 542 m. The Serra de Llevante is a low line of hills running along the east coast.

Natural History: Amateur botanists will be delighted with the variety and accessibility of the island's wild plants – over 1500 types of shrubs, heathers, wild herbs and bright spring flowers. Pines and holm oaks are the most plentiful trees. Annual harvests are taken from the many olive trees, some very old and gnarled, carobs with their heavy seed pods, almond trees which produce a spectacular display of pinky-white blossom in Feb. (as well as producing 70% of Spain's crop) and sweet-smelling citrus trees (mostly in the Sóller valley). Figs and apricots are also widely grown. On warm evenings you'll hear the chirping cicadas. Hares, rabbits and game birds are shot for the pot Oct.-Jan. though the wild mountain goats are protected. There are several species of snake, though all are harmless. See **Bird-watching, Parc Natural de S'Albufera.**

Palma

Palma: The capital city is a stylish, all-year-round destination which offers the island's best choice of sophisticated hotels, restaurants, shopping and entertainment. It is also an important historic and cultural centre and a good base from which to make excursions by public transport to the rest of the island. See BUILDINGS 1, MUSEUMS 1, NIGHTLIFE 1, RESORTS 1, RESTAURANTS 1, SHOPPING 1 & 2, WALKS 1 & 2.

Palma Nova & Magaluf: Against a backdrop of pine-covered hills, hotel, apartment and commercial blocks follow the curves of two wide bays and their golden sandy beaches. Most are geared to giving North Europeans a lot of hectic action and value for money by day and night. Magaluf has one of the island's few casinos as well as a good choice of sports and attractions for children. Portals Vells (see BEACHES) and Cala Figuera (see A-Z) are just two of the pretty wooded coves to the south best reached by boat. See RESORTS 1.

Parc Natural de S'Albufera: This was created in 1985 with the purchase by the Balearics autonomous government of 800 hectares of precious wetlands and sand dunes rescued from the encroachment of tourist developments on the bay of Alcúdia.
As well as the bulrushes and marram grasses which crowd the sides of streams and ditches, plant life includes pine woods and tamarisks, prickly juniper and several species of orchid, among them the rare mirror orchid.
The park's greatest treasure, however, is its rich bird life – over 200 species of native and migratory birds, among them hoopoes, stilts, kestrels and ospreys. Other occasional visitors include the purple heron and the greater flamingo. See EXCURSION 3.

Peguera: This resort has a good range of hotels and apartments, some with exceptional locations, and budget eating places. Scandinavians and Germans outnumber the British here. The resort is well located for hiking, cycling and riding excursions through pretty countryside. See RESORTS 2.

Platja de Canyamel: See Cala Millor.

Pollença

Platjas de Mallorca: See Port d'Alcúdia.

Platjas de Muro: See BEACHES, Ca'n Picafort.

Platjas de Palma: A string of resorts which cater mostly for British and German package tourists, and in high summer are noisy and congested. Ca'n Pastilla's proximity to the airport adds to the noise levels there. Son Veri and Cala Blava are the quieter parts. Good sports amenities are plentiful. *Balnearios* (refreshment and service areas) and children's play areas are spaced along the beach which gets very crowded at Ca'n Pastilla and S'Arenal. There are small coves at either end of the *platja*. See RESORTS 1.

Pollença: An attractive town of narrow streets, it is famous for its Roman bridge, the Calvari steps and its international festival of music (see MUSIC). On show in the cloister and upstairs rooms of the Claustre de Santo Domingo (see MUSEUMS 2) are contemporary sculptures and paintings acquired through the annual international art competition, the Premi de Pollença. The monastery church has a magnificent Baroque altarpiece and some 15thC paintings. See EXCURSION 2.

Portals Nous: See RESORTS 1.

Port d'Alcúdia: The area has comprehensive leisure, sports and entertainment facilities, and is popular and lively, particularly with Germans, in high season. Nearby are Alcúdia and the Parc Natural de S'Albufera (see A-Z). A good choice of boat excursions is available, including exploring small canals by water scooter. The Platjas de Mallorca are a long stretch of beach with fine white sand. See EXCURSION 3, RESORTS 2.

Port d'Andratx: A small fishing village with a now burgeoning tourist industry. It is a good centre for walking or sightseeing by car or boat. The best beach, with some amenities, is at Camp de Mar, which also has the higher-rated hotels and is a popular stop for excursion boats. Another beach can be found at Sant Telm (see BEACHES), with

Porto Cristo

simple accommodation and eating places. Sant Telm faces the bird sanctuary of Dragonera island, another excursion destination. See **RESORTS 2**.

Port de Pollença: This resort and nearby Cala Sant Vicenç and Formentor are popular with British families. Early and late season, and in winter, it's a favourite of the older generation. Rides and walks in the surrounding countryside are rewarded with lovely views and there's a variety of organized trips by boat. Along the horseshoe bay of Pollença, the beaches are long and open or smaller and pine-shaded. At the smaller resort of Sant Vicenç, there's a choice of three beaches (sandy, rocky or pebbly). Platja Formentor (see **BEACHES**) is bordered by pines and there are more intimate coves along the cape. The area's nightlife centres on bars, restaurants and a few discos. Nearby is Pollença (see **A-Z**). See **EXCURSION 2**, **RESORTS 2**.

Port de Sóller: Day-trippers from Palma and elsewhere crowd this attractive resort which is popular with French families. It is a good base for excursions by horse taxi, car or on foot into lovely countryside and dramatic mountain areas. Sa Calobra (see **BEACHES**), Truent and many other pretty coves with tiny beaches can be visited by boat. See **EXCURSION 4**, **RESORTS 2**.

Porto Colom: See **RESORTS 3**.

Porto Cristo: The nearby caves of Drac and Hams (see **CAVES**) are
the principal attraction for day-trippers to this small port. Bigger tourist
development is northwards at S'Illot, Cala Moreia and Sa Coma, which
have better, sandy beaches and are still popular with local people from
nearby villages. To the south, Porto Cristo Novo and Cala Estany have
secluded sandy coves. See **RESORTS 3**.

Porto Cristo Novo: See Porto Cristo.

Porto Petro: See Cala d'Or.

Puigpunyent: A picturesque village with some fine old buildings in
its narrow streets and the mansion of Son Forteza (see **BUILDINGS 2**).

Romans: In 123 BC Mallorca's notoriety as a base for pirates prompt-
ed a successful attack on the island by the Roman commander Quintus
Cecilius Metullus, who covered his boats in skins to repel the hail of
stones from fierce islanders. Palma became a Roman settlement but the
most important centre on the island was Pollentia, now the town of
Alcúdia, where the theatre and several houses have been excavated
(see **EXCURSION 3, MUSEUMS 2**). See **Foners**.

Sa Coma: See Porto Cristo.

Salvator, Ludwig: An Austrian archduke who first visited Mallorca
in the 1860s. From 1872 to 1913 he spent most of his time on the
island and became one of the first publicists of the island's charms
through his nine-volume work *Die Balearen in Wort und Bild*. His mansion at Son Marroig, Deià, is open to the public (see **BUILDINGS 2**).

Sant Agustí: See Cala Major.

Santa Ponça: Similar to Palma Nova and Magaluf (see **A-Z**) but a
slightly quieter pace. It has a golf course and up-market areas near the
smart marina. The gently sloping beach with good sand is well served
with amenities. See **RESORTS 1**.

Sant Telm: See BEACHES, **Port d'Andratx**.

S'Arenal: See **Platjas de Palma**.

Serra, Junipero (1713-84): A Franciscan friar, born in Petra of humble origins, who left for the New World in 1749. He helped to set up many of the mission stations (named after the statues of saints in his home town's San Bernardino church) which later grew into the towns and cities of California. His house at Petra in c/ Junipero Serra is open to the public 0900-2000, while visits to the museum at c/ Barracal 6, Petra can be arranged, tel: 561149.

S'Illot: See **Porto Cristo**.

Sóller: A market town set among citrus groves below the island's highest peaks and made busy by day-trippers on the Palma–Sóller railway line. Its main square has a Modernista (see **A-Z**) bank and church façade. See EXCURSION 4.

Son Vida: See RESORTS 1.

Talaias: *Atalaya* in Castilian. Medieval watchtowers along the coast from which warnings of approaching pirates and invaders were given. Ses Animas, between Estellencs and Banyalbufar, is an accessible example, while the ruins of the Talaia d'Alcúdia are reached by a steep climb from the Ermità de la Victoria, near Alcúdia.

Talaiots: *Talayots* in Castilian. Stone towers built from about 1300 to 100 BC in settlements like Capicorp Vell, Llucmajor or Ses Païsses, Artà. Remains of an estimated 200 *talaiot* settlements are scattered around the island. See **Bronze Age**.

Valldemossa: This village of narrow, cobbled streets and some elegant houses rises up a rugged hill, and is dominated by the monastery of Reial Cartoixa (Real Cartuja) (see BUILDINGS 2). The monastery visit includes the 18thC church with frescoes by Bayeu, the Prior's Cell with paintings and an extensive library, the refectory with a ceramics collection, pharmacy, municipal museum (see **MUSEUMS 2**) and the cells occupied by Chopin (see **A-Z**) and George Sand, where a delightful little garden has views over the valley. The same ticket also gives admission to the adjacent Palau del Rei Sanxo, an early-14thC palace built by King Jaume II of Mallorca for his son Sanxo, and a short piano recital. Also of interest in Valldemossa are the Gothic parish church and, across from it, the birthplace of Mallorca's only native saint, Catalina Tomás (0930-1300, 1500-1830).

Windmills: These are a characteristic feature of the Mallorcan landscape and often have brightly-painted sails. The smaller of the two types of *molís* are those which pump water from the plentiful subterranean supply with which the island is blessed. More solidly built, of stone, and comprising three floors, are the old grain mills, some of which have now been converted into homes. You'll probably catch sight of some on the way to and from Palma airport. Some have also been preserved in Palma's Es Jonquet area (see **WALK 2**).

Accidents & Breakdowns: In the event of an accident or breakdown you can summon help by dialling 009 (no coins required). There are SOS telephones on major roads. The police (see **A-Z**) must be informed as soon as possible after an accident. If you hire a car, check the company's conditions and procedures before you set off. See **Consulates**, **Driving**, **Emergency Numbers**.

Accommodation: Mallorca has Europe's densest concentration of holiday accommodation. For instance, it offers more beds in hotels and apartments than the whole of Greece. Only a few places have so far aimed at the top end of the international market and in this category the Hotel Formentor is the most outstanding. There are no *paradores* (high-class, State-run hotels) but a number of beautiful old mansions and country houses have been converted into hotels, of which the best-known is La Residencia in Deià.

Officially rated accommodation: Hotels (H) are rated one- to five-star, with *gran lujo* the very top rating. An *hotel apartamento* (HA) offers full hotel services with accommodation in apartments. An *hotel residencia* (HR) does not have a full restaurant. *Hostales* (H^S) are much like hotels, usually with more modest facilities, and are rated one to three stars. *Fondas* (inns) and *casas de huéspedes* (guesthouses) offer the most basic accommodation. *Apartamentos turísticos* (AT) are rated from one to four keys, have self-catering facilities and usually require a minimum stay of one week. Camping is classified upwards from 1st to 3rd category. There are nine *ciudades de vacaciones* or sun clubs with most accommodation in bungalows, operating April-Oct., which have comprehensive sports and entertainment facilities. A booklet listing all types of accommodation is published each year by the Spanish Tourist Board (see **Tourist Information**). See **Camping**, **Monasteries**, **Self-catering**, **Youth Hostels**.

Airport: Son Sant Joan airport is 10 km west along the motorway from Palma. Terminal A is for scheduled airlines and Terminal B for charter flights. Facilities include a bank, tourist office, hotel booking service, car-hire desks, post office, baggage porters, souvenir and duty-free shops, and bars. Bus 17 links with Plaça Espanya in Palma every

30 min. Metered taxis are relatively inexpensive, though there are supplements for the airport journey and for baggage.

Useful numbers: Flight enquiries, tel: 264624; tourist desk, tel: 260803; hotel desk, tel: 262649 (Ultramar Express).

Baby-sitters: Many hotel and apartment complexes operate a daytime care and entertainment programme and a room-listening service at night. In some small places a member of the family or staff may babysit. You can also ask locally about *canguros* (professional baby-sitters) and *guarderías* (crèches). See **CHILDREN**, **Children**.

Banks: See **Currency**, **Money**, **Opening Times**.

Beaches: There are no 'undiscovered' beaches on the island. The most secluded, good beaches are in the northeast and southeast, reached on foot or by boat. Except during freak conditions, the popular beaches are all very safe with little tidal variation. The water in Palma bay can occasionally become polluted. See **BEACHES**, **RESORTS 1-3**.

Best Buys: These include leather goods, artificial pearls, embroidered linen goods, woven-grass items, ceramics and carved olivewood. The island's liqueurs, *hierbas secas*, *hierbas dulces* and *palo*, make good presents. See **SHOPPING 1-3**, **Markets**.

Bicycle & Motorcycle Hire: Hire facilities are widely available in the resorts. Cycles without gears start from around 500 ptas per day. Mountain bikes, mopeds and motorcycles are more expensive. Some resorts have cycle lanes. For motorcycles and mopeds, check that your holiday insurance does not exclude cover of any accidents while riding one of these. Minimum age for mopeds is 16; for motorcycles over 75cc it's 18. A crash-helmet is required for the latter, and recommended for both.

Bird-watching: The island's rich bird life – native and migratory – makes Mallorca an attractive destination for bird-watchers. Specialist publications in English are available on the island. The best areas are the Parc Natural de S'Albufera (see **EXCURSION 3**, **A-Z**) in the north and the salt flats of Salines de Llevant, near Colònia de Sant Jordi in the south. In both, the range of birds includes hoopoes, stilts, heron and, occasionally, the greater flamingo.

Buses: A comprehensive network of scheduled bus services from Palma to most towns and resorts, and connecting between the resort areas, provides an inexpensive means of getting around. Most services operate from Palma's Plaça Espanya or nearby streets. Other principal stops are at Plaça Joan Carles I (Illetas, Portals Nous), Plaça Reina (Platja de Palma) and La Rambla (Andratx). Bus timetables are displayed at bus stops, and are available at tourist offices and Plaça Espanya. See **Excursions**.

Cameras & Photography: The island is very photogenic. Make allowances for bright sunlight and glare. Because of midday haze, early morning and late afternoon are the best times for panoramic shots. Keep film and cameras out of the heat and away from sand and sea. Do not attempt to photograph policemen, or military personnel and installations. Photography, or use of flashlight, is not allowed in some tourist attractions. Film, developing and printing are generally more expensive in Spain than in other European countries. Rapid processing places give the standard quality service.

Camping: There are two official sites: Camping Platja Blava, Platja de Muro, tel: 537863 (1st category); and Club San Pedro, Colònia de San Pedro, tel: 589023 (3rd category). Off-site camping is not encouraged and is never allowed on beaches, in mountain areas or along dry river beds. Always ask permission from private owners.

Car Hire: All the big international firms operate in Mallorca, either directly or with Spanish associates. Scheduled airlines offer 'fly-drive' schemes. Holiday operators have car-hire offers. Smaller, local firms, whose leaflets may also be picked up at hotels and tourist offices, usually have lower rates. Check if your hotel has any special arrangements. It is worthwhile looking out for special deals and term discounts. Don't forget to compare all-inclusive costs as insurance and mileage charges can pump up the bill considerably. Insurance includes third party and a bail bond but it is also advisable to take comprehensive insurance, including collision damage waiver. Remember, value-added tax (IVA) is 12%. See **Driving**.

Chemists: *Farmacias* (green cross sign) are chemist shops where prescriptions can be obtained. A notice on the door or in newspapers will give the address of the nearest on-duty chemist outside normal hours. Prescription medicines are relatively inexpensive. Obtain and keep all receipts for subsequent submission to your insurers. See **Health**.

Children: Like most Mediterranean people, Mallorcans display fondness for and tolerance of children. They're made very welcome almost anywhere and at any time. Beyond the safe, sandy beaches there are lots of facilities for children. See CHILDREN, **Baby-sitters**.

Climate: The mild Mediterranean climate is favourably affected by local features. Sea breezes modify heat and humidity at the height of summer. Relatively high, westerly mountains protect the south from the colder winter winds. Waters along shallow beaches are quickly heated by the sun. Because the island has a varied landscape, there's a noticeable variation in a day's weather from place to place. If it's too hot and sultry by the sea, you'll find that a short journey away the mountains will be cool and shady. If it's cloudy on the north coast, it may well be sunny along the south, and vice versa. In Palma temperatures seldom exceed 36°C or drop below 5°C. Its average temperature and rainfall are: spring 23.6°C, 34 mm; summer 30.3°C, 54mm; autumn 21°C, 85 mm; winter 16°C, 120 mm. There is sunshine on about 300 days each year.

Complaints: Places of accommodation, restaurants and petrol stations have to keep *hojas de reclamación* (complaints forms in triplicate). If your complaint is about price, you must first pay the bill before requesting the forms. After the form is filled in, one copy is retained by you and another is sent to the tourism department of the regional government. This is a valuable consumer protection facility which should not be abused by using it for petty complaints.

Consulates:
UK – Plaça Mayor 3d, Palma, tel: 712445.
USA – Avinguda Jaume III 26, Palma, tel: 722660.

Conversion Chart:

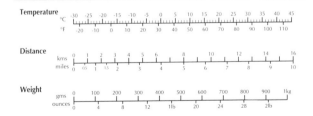

Crime & Theft: Compared with many resorts, crime against tourists is rare on Mallorca. Deposit valuables in the hotel safe; ensure that your room is locked when you leave; carry handbags, etc. on the off-street side; walk in a group; use licensed taxis. If you have been the subject of a crime, try to find witnesses, and report the incident to the police (see **A-Z**). Get a copy of your statement for insurance purposes.

Currency: The peseta (pta) is Spain's monetary unit.
Notes – 10,000, 5000, 2000, 1000.
Coins – 500, 200, 100, 50, 25, 10, 5, 1.
See **Money**.

Customs Allowances:

UK/EC	Cigarettes	Cigarillos	Cigars	Tobacco	Still Table Wine	Spirits/Liqueurs	Fortified Wine	Additional Still Table Wine	Perfume	Toilet Water	Gifts & Souvenirs
Duty Free	200	100	50	250 g	2 *l*	1 *l*	2 *l*	2 *l*	60 cc/ml	250 cc/ml	£32
Duty Paid	800	400	200	1 kg	90 *l**	10 *l*	20 *l*				

* Of which no more than 60 l should be sparkling wine.

Since 1 Jan. 1993 restrictions on allowances for duty-paid goods brought into the UK from any EC country have been abolished. Travellers are now able to buy goods, including alcoholic drinks and tobacco, paying duty and VAT in the EC country where the goods are purchased. However, duty-paid goods should be for the traveller's own use and carried by him personally. Whereas previously there were either-or options, travellers can now bring back the sum of the goods in the duty-paid column.

Disabled People: Although facilities for people with disabilities are still insufficient, the island compares favourably with much of the rest of Europe, with many new developments having wheelchair access and suitable toilets. Make full enquiries at travel agents or holiday operators before booking. The main association for people with disabilities is ASPROM, c/ Pascual Ribot 6a, Palma, tel: 289052. For special needs on public transport, tel: 295700. See **Health**, **Insurance**.

Drinks: Although tap water is safe, foreigners usually fare better by sticking to bottled *agua mineral* (bottled water), *con gas* (carbonated) or *sin gas* (still). *Te* (tea) is usually served *con limón* (with a slice of lemon). *Infusión de manzanilla* is refreshing camomile tea. *Horchata* is a milk-like drink made from groundnuts. *Granizado* is iced, fresh fruit juice. Coffee (*café*) comes *solo* (black) or *con leche* (with milk). Chocolate, thick and creamy, is drunk for breakfast or as a nightcap. Various qualities of Spanish and imported beer (*cerveza*) are available. *Una caña* (draught beer) is usually lower priced. *Sangría* is of varying strength and is made from ice, soda water, red wine, brandy, fruit and juices. Sherry is called *jerez* and can be fino (pale dry), amontillado (medium) or oloroso (heavier and sweeter). *Coñac* (brandy) varies from rough to fine (10 year or older *reservas*). *Palo*, flavoured with crushed almond shells, is one of the island's many liqueurs. See **Wines**.

Driving: You need the following with you when driving: passport, current driving licence (international or EC), vehicle registration document, third-party insurance document and bail bond (usually covered by car-hire agreement document), spare headlight, sidelight and rearlight bulbs, red warning triangle (if you're going on motorways). Minimum age is 18. Drive on the right. Overtake on the left. Give way to traffic coming from the left, especially at roundabouts, unless it's clearly marked that your road has priority. Never cross a solid white line to overtake or turn left. Always use indicators before overtaking or turning. Speed limits are: 60 kph on most urban roads; 90 kph on other roads where indicated; 100 kph on main roads; and 120 kph on motorways. Seat belts must be worn in front seats outside urban areas. No hooting in urban areas unless in an emergency. Lights must be dipped

for oncoming traffic. Don't drink and drive (permitted maximum is 0.8 g alcohol per 1000 cc). Penalties for offences can be severe and include prison terms. Take care when driving on Mallorca's mountain roads, which can be steep and narrow with a number of tight hairpin bends. See **Accidents & Breakdowns**, **Parking**, **Petrol**.

Drugs: Possession of drugs is illegal and bringing drugs into the country is subject to harsh penalties. Previously liberal policies have hardened to prevent drugs, and the associated crime, becoming a problem.

Eating Out: In the resorts there are plenty of restaurants serving British, German, Chinese and all kinds of fast food. Around harbours there are generally a number of places to sample fresh local fish and seafood. Other restaurants specializing in traditional Mallorquin cooking are definitely worth trying. The grading of restaurants from one to five forks reflects the standard of facilities and generally also gives an indication of price but cannot be taken as a guide to quality. Mealtimes on Mallorca are usually breakfast until 1100, lunch 1300-1500 and dinner from 2030, but places which cater for tourists often start lunch and dinner earlier. Menus are in Castilian Spanish, usually with English and/or German translations, with Mallorquin used only for the names of local specialities. The *menu del dia* offers two or three courses with bread and wine or beer at low cost. See RESTAURANTS 1-3, **Food**.

Electricity: 220/225 V. Round-pin, two-point plugs. Wiring is colour-coded to international standard. Older buildings may still have 110/125 V supplies.

Emergency Numbers: Tel: 091 or 092 for the Policía Nacional (see **Police**). Concentrate on giving your location, nature of the emergency and saying what other services may be required. Emergency ambulance services can also be called direct, tel: 722222, and the fire brigade on 751234.

Events: Most local tourist offices have monthly or quarterly lists of coming events. Look out for special leaflets there and in hotels advertising specific events or festivals. See MUSIC, **Festivals**, **Newspapers**, **What's On**.

Excursions: For those who prefer not to drive, a huge variety of bus tours is available. Tours leave from Palma and main resorts and are bookable at some hotels or any travel agency. The range includes a day trip round the island, or major sightseeing destinations such as caves (see **CAVES**). Most include at least one stop at a craft workshop. Evening tours are available to the many dinner and show venues (see **NIGHTLIFE 2**). Boat excursions are a good way of exploring Mallorca's magnificent coastline and visiting inaccessible beaches or islands such as Dragonera and Cabrera. A boat excursions leaflet is available from tourist offices.

Ferries: There are regular connections from Palma throughout the year to Ibiza, Barcelona, Valencia and Mahón (Menorca). A daily hydrojet operates to Ibiza, June-Sep., with connections to Sète (France), Nov.-Mar., Genoa (Italy) and the Canary Islands. For information, contact Ucona Transmediterránea, Moll Vell, Palma, tel: 726740.

Festivals: Local festivals are where the island's traditions, costumes and folklore are best observed. Courtship dances, the bolero, jota and *parado*, are accompanied by *xeremies* (bagpipes), drums, guitars and castanets. Women's costumes consist of a white lace headdress and brightly-coloured skirt, while the men wear distinctive baggy breeches. *2 July:* Pilgrimage to the Ermità de la Victoria, near Alcúdia; *28 July:* Carro Triumfal, Valldemossa, in honour of the island saint, Catalina Tomás or Sor Tomasseta; *2 Aug.:* Mare de Déu dels Angels, Pollença, with fireworks and mock battles between Moors and Christians; *28 Aug:* Sant Agustí, Felanitx, with medieval dances by *cavallets* (youngsters dressed in horse costumes); *Last Sun. in Sep.:* Festa d'es Vermar, Binissalem, to celebrate the grape harvest. A leaflet with details of local festivals is available from tourist offices.

Food: Traditional Mallorcan food is delicious and its specialities are worth searching out. *Tapas* (snacks) may be spicy, as chili is often added. Many bars serve these tempting appetizers, ranging from olives, nuts or crisps to small and tasty portions of meats, seafoods, omelettes, salads or vegetables. Some are served hot. *Raciones* are larger portions of the same things. Other tasty snacks are: *cocos*, like small pizzas filled with vegetables, fish or something sweet; *empanadas*, meat and vegetable pasty; *sobrasada*, *botifarro* and *llongarusa*, types of highly-seasoned, cured pork sausages, delicious on *pa pagès*, simple bread; and *pa amb oli*, bread spread with fresh tomato, seasoned with salt and olive oil. Main meals often begin with *sopas mallorquinas*, vegetable soups thickened with bread, sometimes with pork added, or *tremp*, a summer salad of tomato, green pepper and onion. Fish and seafood ranges from simply grilled fresh sardines to *calderata langosta*, lobster pieces in tomato sauce. A number of traditional dishes use eels, a favourite island delicacy. They include *greixonera d'anguiles* (eel casserole) and *espinagada* (spicy eel and vegetable pie). Rice is grown at Muro and Sa Pobla (La Puebla), from where the savoury rice dish *arròs brut* originates. *Tumbet*, tomatoes, aubergines and potatoes fried in oil, is served either as a starter or with meat or fish as a main course. Other main courses include: *frit de mallorquin*, fried, spiced innards of pork or lamb; *lechona asada*, roast suckling pig; and *escaldums*, chicken casserole with potato and almonds. *Ensaimadas* are delicious sweet pastries eaten at breakfast or mid-morning, or filled with cream, almonds or fruit as a dessert. *Galletes d'oli* are salted biscuits made in Inca. See **RESTAURANTS 1-3**, **Eating Out**.

Health: Drinks are inexpensive, measures are generous and the heat generates a thirst, and alcoholic overindulgence is one of the biggest health hazards for visitors. Sunburn is painful and sunstroke is very dangerous. Pace your exposure to the sun, use high-filter creams for the first few days and wear a hat. Drink one of the bottled waters (*agua mineral*) and stick to it. Avoid having ice, too many salads, mayonnaise and any place whose standards of hygiene look dubious. If your digestion is feeling the strain, eat simple vegetable dishes, tortillas, chicken or plainly grilled fish. Health foods are available from *herboristerías* in Palma and many resorts. First-aid preparations and patent medicines are sold in *farmacias* (see **Chemists**). Unfortunately, mosquitoes can be numerous, particularly in the north around the bay of Alcúdia and in the south around Colònia de Sant Jordi, but plug-in machines can be effective during the night. There are several types of snake but all are harmless. On Mallorca, your hotel will assist in calling a doctor or making an appointment with doctors or dentists. Your consulate (see **A-Z**) may provide lists of medical practitioners. You will be required to pay for each visit or consultation. Emergency cases are usually accepted at both public and private clinics or hospitals. Unless you have obtained a card entitling you to Spanish public health services, you will be charged for these services in the same way as by private clinics. On presentation of your insurance policy, practitioners and clinics may accept waiting for payment of large bills from the insurers. See **Disabled People**, **Insurance**.

Insurance: You should take out travel insurance covering you against theft and loss of property and money, as well as medical expenses, for the duration of your stay. Your travel agent should be able to recommend a suitable policy. See **Crime & Theft**, **Driving**, **Health**.

Language: Since the creation of the autonomous government, the Gobern Balear, in 1983, both Mallorquin and Castilian Spanish are the official languages of Mallorca. Mallorquin is a variant of Catalan, the language of the Spanish mainland from Catalunya to Valencia. Among themselves, islanders speak Mallorquin but they all also speak Castilian and many have learned English, German or French. All place and street

names have reverted to their Mallorquin forms and in schools
Mallorquin is increasingly being introduced. Menus, newspapers and
most books are still in Castilian. Campaigns for increased use of
Mallorquin or Catalan have led to new literature and theatre with government support on the island. Visitors may notice grafitti in support of
the campaign. For example, signs for Palma are often daubed Ciutat
(meaning 'city'), the old Mallorquin name.

NOTE: In keeping with the policy of the autonomous government of the
Balearic Islands and their tourist offices, all street and place names in
this guidebook are given in their Mallorquin (Catalan) forms. Older maps
and guidebooks give the Castilian Spanish versions. Where confusion
may arise, the Castilian name is here given in brackets after the
Mallorquin.

Laundries: Hotels have laundry and dry-cleaning services. A *lavan-
dería* (laundry) or *tintorería* (dry cleaner), of which there are many, is
likely to be cheaper. They usually charge by weight and need a minimum of 24 hr.

Lost Property: If you have lost something, tell the hall porter or a
person in charge wherever you are staying. Lost property offices are usually at the local Ajuntament (town hall). In Palma, it's on Plaça Cort. If
the loss is serious, report it to the local police and get a copy of your
statement. Promptly advise credit card companies, issuers of traveller's
cheques and, if your passport is lost, your consulate (see **A-Z**). See
Insurance.

Markets: Palma's most famous market is the *barabillo* (*rastrillo* in
Castilian) or flea market held 0800-1400 Sat. On Fri. & Sat. (1000-1400)
there is a crafts market in Plaça Major. The fish market, Llotja del Peix,
Moll de Pescadors, is a fascinating and busy place Mon.-Fri. am. Other
food and general markets are at Plaça Olivar, Plaça Pere Garau, Plaça
Navegació, c/ Manuel Azaña 44 (Polígòn de Llevant), Avinguda Sant
Ferran and c/ Joan Crespí on Mon.-Sat. am. Outside Palma, every town
and village has a market, usually in and around the main square, once or
twice a week. A leaflet listing them all is available from the tourist office.

Santuari de Sant Salvador

Monasteries: Accommodation is available in some of the island's monasteries and sanctuaries. It is inexpensive and ranges from the *hostal*-like facilities to be found at Lluc, tel: 517025, to the spartan cells at Sant Salvador, tel: 580656 (see **BUILDINGS 2**). Others include Nostra Senyora de Cura, Randa, tel: 660994, and Ermità Puig de Maria, Pollença (no advance booking).

Money: Banks offer the best exchange rate. It is essential to present your passport for any transaction involving traveller's cheques. The major international credit and charge cards are widely accepted, as are traveller's cheques in any west European currency or US dollars and Eurocheques supported by a valid card. Most cashpoint machines accept Visa, Access and Eurocheque cards, and have an English-language facility. See **Currency**, **Opening Times**.

Newspapers: *El Día 16 de Balares*, *Diario de Mallorca*, *Última Hora* and *Baleares* are locally-published daily newspapers in Castilian Spanish. The Barcelona edition of *El País*, Spain's newspaper with the highest international reputation, is available. *Cambio 16* is the top weekly news magazine. The English-language *Mallorca Daily Bulletin* and *The Reader* (weekly) give some coverage of international, Spanish and island news. Leading foreign newspapers and magazines are widely available, many on their day of publication. For classified adverts listing services, hire facilities, etc., look for the weekly *Trueque*. See **What's On**.

Nightlife: There's no shortage of nightlife on the island. Large hotels and apartment complexes often have their own discos and late-night bars, with many more to choose from in most resorts. Palma and the bay of Palma resorts have the greatest concentration and variety. Spain has an active and adventurous film industry. Most foreign films are dubbed. Showings in the original version with Castilian subtitles are advertised as 'v.o.' The first showing in Palma's cinemas is usually at 1530, the last about 2230. Check for cinema shows in tourist complexes. See **NIGHTLIFE 1-3**.

Nudism: Women go topless on any beach and poolside. Both sexes strip totally on Platja Mago and Platja Es Trenc, and in some secluded coves. A few hotels have terraces for nude sunbathing. See **BEACHES**.

Opening Times:
Shops – 0900/1000-1300/1400, 1600/1730-1930/2100 Mon.-Fri. Sat. is half-day closing. In the high season some shops may stay open later to take advantage of the tourist trade; in winter some close earlier.
Galerías Preciados department store – 1000-2100 Mon.-Sat.
Supermarkets – 0900-2200 Mon.-Sat. (summer), 0900-2000 (winter).
Business offices – 0900-1400, 1630-1900.
Government offices – 1100-1300 Mon.-Fri.
Banks – 0900-1400 Mon.-Fri., 0900-1300 Sat.

Orientation: The Balearic Islands of Mallorca, Menorca, Ibiza and Formentera lie off mainland Spain's east coast and are the last outcrops in the Mediterranean mountain range which runs through southern Spain. They form the Comunitat Autonoma de les Illes Balears, one of Spain's autonomous regions. Mallorca, largest of the group, is roughly 100 km at its widest (east–west) and 75 km at its longest (north–south). It is delightfully varied geographically, with high, rugged mountains, a rich agricultural plain and an indented coastline of 500 km, along which lie pine-fringed beaches. Palma de Mallorca, where over half the 600,000 Mallorquins live, is the historic but sophisticated capital.

Parking: Parking prohibitions are usually clearly marked by painted kerbstones and signs. A leaflet available from car-hire firms and tourist offices explains Palma's restricted parking system known as ORA. See **Driving**.

Passports & Customs: Tourists holding a valid passport of a EC country or of the USA and Canada do not require a visa to enter Spain. Those with Australian, New Zealand, South African, Japanese and some other passports should obtain a visa from a Spanish consulate. See **Customs Allowances**.

Petrol: Petrol (*gasolina*) is available as *súper* (4 star) and *normal* (2 star), *sin plomo* (unleaded) or *con plomo* (leaded). Diesel is *gas-oil* or *gaseolo*. In main towns and resorts petrol stations are open 0600-2200. They may close or have reduced hours on Sun. A number on main routes (including the one at the airport) are open 24 hr. See **Driving**.

Police: The Policía Nacional are the tough, smart-looking men and women in khaki and brown uniforms and berets who walk the streets in twos and patrol in white and tan vehicles. Report any crime to them and make a formal statement at their *comisaria*. Their HQ is at c/ Friedrich Holderlin 8, Palma, tel: 280400. The Policía Municipal (blue uniforms, white or blue cars) deal mainly with urban traffic and enforcing municipal regulations. In some resorts they may be assisted by corps of Policía Turistica in the high season. You'll see the Guardia Civil (green uniforms and tricorn hats or soft caps) at immigration and customs posts and patrolling roads, the coastline and rural areas. See **Crime & Theft**, **Emergency Numbers**.

Post Offices: Post offices (*correos*) are open for general business 0900-1300, 1600-1900 Mon.-Fri., and Sat. half day. In some resorts they may be in caravans and only open during the main season. In Palma, the main post office is on Plaça Constitución. You can have mail addressed here: Name, Lista de Correos, Plaça Constitución, Palma de Mallorca, Spain. Take your passport as identification when collecting. Stamps (*sellos*) can also be bought from hotels or tobacconists (*estancos* or *tabacos*). Postboxes are yellow. Slots marked *extranjero* are for mail going beyond Spain.

Public Holidays: 1 Jan., 6 Jan., 1 May, 24 June, 25 July, 15 Aug., 12 Oct., 1 Nov., 8 Dec., 25 Dec., 31 Dec. and on the variable feast days of Good Fri., Easter Mon. and Corpus Christi. Additionally, towns and villages have their particular fiesta days which are also public holidays.

Rabies: Still exists or is considered a threat throughout Spain, as in other parts of Europe. Take the precaution of having all animal bites seen by a doctor.

Coves del Drac

Railways: There are two rail links, both narrow gauge, operating in Mallorca. The Palma–Inca line, operating from Plaça Espanya, has trains at least once an hour, with stops including Santa Maria, Consell and Binissalem. The Palma–Sóller line from c/ Eusebi Estada, next to Plaça Espanya, is popular with tourists and has around five trains per day each way (see **EXCURSION 4**). Both lines run seven days a week. Timetables are available from stations and tourist offices. For Palma–Inca information, tel: 752245, and Palma–Sóller, tel: 752051.

Religious Services: A full list of services in English is available at tourist offices.

Self-catering: One of the fastest-growing areas of the tourist market, self-catering accommodation can vary from apartment complexes attached to large hotels in busy resorts to luxuriously converted *fincas* (farmhouses) in idyllic rural settings. Agencies and individuals advertise in the holiday sections of quality newspapers in Britain. *Agencias de alquiler* on the island also offer properties to let, mostly for a minimum period of one month.

Shopping: See **SHOPPING 1-3**, **Best Buys**, **Markets**, **Opening Times**.

Smoking: Smoking is not permitted on public transport in Mallorca, nor in the auditoriums of theatres. In general, however, smoking is still widely tolerated, even in many shops.

Sports:
Participatory sports:
Fishing – Enquire at local tourist offices about licences, the best spots for rock fishing, organized trips, boat and tackle hire. Sole, sea bass, *denton*, dorado and sea bream are some varieties. The reservoirs of Gorg Blau and Cuver have trout and carp.
Golf – Golfing holidays on the island are becoming increasingly popular. There are currently 12 courses, with more under construction. The majority (Bendinat, Santa Ponça, Pomente, Son Vida, etc.) are close to Palma but there are also courses at Pollença, S'Horta (near Cala d'Or),

Canyamel and Costa dels Pins in the north and east. Many of the courses are beautifully situated and have good facilities, which include
swimming pools and other sports. Bendinat, Pollença, S'Horta and
Costa dels Pins are currently only nine holes. Prices tend to be high by
comparison with many British clubs. A booklet with characteristics and
facilities is available from tourist offices.

Horse riding – At a *club hípico* or *rancho* you'll find horses for hire, riding instruction and group excursions. The best facilities and terrain for
convenient, even-ground trekking are at east coast (Cala d'Or) and
north coast resorts.

Tennis – With some 25 tennis clubs and many courts at hotels, apartments, vacation villages, golf and other sports clubs, there are plenty of
places to play. Many courts have floodlights. Details can be obtained
from local tourist offices.

Many other sports can be practised on the island: scuba diving, flying,
hang-gliding, parachute-jumping, billiards, bowling, squash, table tennis. You can go and watch football, basketball and pelota matches, as
well as cycle, horse-trotting and dog races. Details can be obtained
from local tourist offices and newspapers. See **Water Sports**.

Taxis: These are inexpensive by international comparison. They're
free when showing a *libre* sign on the windscreen and a small green
light on the roof. A list of supplements which may be added to the
metered fare is shown in the cab. Taxis without meters charge officially-

fixed fares. Fares are higher after 2100 and at weekends. It's always wise to get an idea of what your journey is going to cost and check that the meter has been switched on. See **Tipping**.

Telephones & Telegrams: Hotels tend to add a big margin to the cost of communications services. Telephone: Area code is 971 (delete the 9 if you're calling from outside Spain). Cheap rate is 2200-0800. Coin-operated booths require 5, 25 and 100 pta coins. Codes for Spanish provinces and other countries are given in the booths. For local calls, dial the number only. For international calls, after the dial tone, dial 07, wait for the second dial tone, then dial the country code plus area code (exclude initial 0) plus the number. At the Telefónica offices in Palma (Avinguda Jaume III 20 and c/ Constitución 1) and cabins in many resorts during the season, payment is easier (after the call) and assistance is available. Telex and fax are available at main post offices and business services bureaux. Telegrams can be sent by telephone on 722000 or from post offices. See **Emergency Numbers**.

Television & Radio: The national television company TVE presents two channels in Castilian. Between 1230 and 1300 June-Sep. Channel 2 features news in French, English and German. TV3 is a Catalan channel. Increasingly, hotel, apartment and villa complexes are offering cable and satellite channels. Around 20 radio stations are available on AM and FM. Try 103.2 FM for English broadcasts. Overseas services of some other countries can be picked up on medium or short wave.

Time Difference: 1 hr ahead of GMT and BST.

Tipping: Although it may not be shown separately, a service charge is included on all hotel and restaurant bills. But it's still the practice to leave 5-10% in restaurants and to tip hotel staff for special services. At the bar, leave a token tip, and 5-10% for table service. Taxi drivers, hairdressers and tour guides usually get around 10%. Lavatory attendants, doormen, shoeshines and car-parking attendants should be tipped 25-100 ptas.

Toilets: Few and far between. Choose a bar or café, use its facilities, then – though it's not obligatory – have something to drink there.

Tourist Information: There are Spanish national tourist offices in most capitals and major cities throughout the world. In Britain, contact the Spanish Tourist Office, 57 St. James's Street, London SW1A 1LD, tel: 071-4990901. On the island, tourist offices (OIT) are operated by the autonomous government and by municipal authorities.
In Palma there are OITs at: Airport, tel: 260803; Avinguda Jaume III 10, tel: 712216; c/ Santo Domingo 11, tel: 724090; and Plaça Espanya (cabin), tel: 711527.
Other OITs on the island are: Ca's Català, Ctra Andratx s/n, tel: 402739; Magaluf, Roulotte, tel: 681126; Peguera, Roulotte, tel: 687083; Cala Ratjada, Plaça dels Mariners, tel: 563033; Port de Pollença, c/ Miquel Capllonch, tel: 534666; Porto Cristo, c/ Gual 31a, tel: 570168; Port d'Alcúdia, Edifici Xara s/n, tel: 546639; Ca'n Picafort, Plaça Gabriel Roca 6, tel: 527253; Cala Millor, c/ Fetjet 4, tel: 585864, and Parc de la Mar 2, tel: 585409; Sóller, Plaça de Sa Constitució 1, tel: 630200; Port de Sóller, c/ Canónigo Oliver, tel: 630101; Cala d'Or, Avinguda Cala Llonga, tel: 657463; Colònia de Sant Jordi, c/ Doctor Barraquer 5, tel: 655437; and Valldemossa, Reial Cartoixa (Real Cartuja), tel: 612106. OIT caravans often visit smaller resorts and villages and set up on the seafront or in the main square.

Transport: See **Airport, Buses, Ferries, Railways, Taxis**.

Traveller's Cheques: See **Money**.

Walking: For many visitors the number of delightful walks which can be taken on the island is top among its attractions. They vary from short, gentle strolls to arduous whole-day treks. A leaflet entitled *20 Hiking Excursions on the Island of Mallorca* is available from tourist offices and there are also several specialist publications. Never walk alone, don't be too ambitious, wear sensible shoes and a hat, and take sun and wind protection, food and drink.

Mending fishing nets

Water Sports: With 30 *clubs náuticos* and their 10,000 berths, plus many private marinas, Mallorca is a proven favourite of the yachting fraternity. Specialist holiday operators offer sailing 'packages' and yachts can be chartered locally. Your regular yachting magazine is likely to have advertisements. Lessons in dinghy sailing, water-skiing and windsurfing are available in marinas and on many beaches. There's no shortage of places hiring boats and gear, as well as pedalos and open canoes. See **Sports**.

What's On: Look for leaflets and posters at your hotel, tourist offices and travel agents. Billboards advertise events. See **Events**, **Newspapers**.

Wines: *Vino* is *tinto* (red), *blanco* (white) or *rosado* (rosé) – *vi negre*, *blanc* or *rosaso* in Mallorquin. Binissalem produces all three and Felanitx a small quantity of white wines. Although not of an extremely high quality, these wines make palatable table wines. For quality wines, choose one from Spain's *denominaciones de origen*, officially demarcated and controlled wine-growing areas. The Catalan *cavas*, champagne-method sparkling wines, are widely available, as are other quality wines such as Rioja and Penedés. Many restaurants will have a *vino de la casa* (house wine).

Youth Hostels: Alberg Juvenil de Platja de Palma, c/ Costa Brava 13 (c/ Balneario 4), Platja de Palma, tel: 260892; Alberg Juvenil d'Alcúdia 'La Victoria', Ctra Cap de Pinar s/n, Alcúdia, tel: 545698/395. For full details and advance bookings, contact TIVE, c/ Venerable Jeroni Antich 5, Palma, tel: 711785.

Estellencs

This book was produced using QuarkXPress™
and Adobe Illustrator™ on Apple Macintosh™
computers and output to separated film
on a Linotronic™ 300 Imagesetter

Text: Hilary Macartney with additional
contributions by George Kean
Photography: Jan Kruse
Electronic Cartography: Susan Harvey Design
and Iain Robinson (1, 24, 26, 28)

First published 1990 Second Edition 1993
Reprinted 1994
Copyright © HarperCollins Publishers
Published by HarperCollins Publishers
Printed in Italy by Amadeus S.p.A.
ISBN 0 00 470036-8